Getting into the Green Zone:

Secrets to a Life of Optimal Health and Happiness

Understanding a New Concept of Health and Learning how to Achieve it Now.

Dedication

To My Favorite Person

You Will Always be The Love of My Life

This book is just as much yours as it is mine.

Thank You for inspiring me for so many years.

Preface

As I brought this book to light, most people gave me the feedback that it would be a great book for the aging population. But while it is definitely great reading for the elderly, I endeavor to promote this book to all ages because utilizing the principles in this book will most greatly benefit younger adults. I decided to write this book because I only wish someone had told me these principles when I was young. These are things that should be taught in school but are not. Had someone taught me these crucial concepts I probably would have modeled and approached my life in an entirely different manner. This is not to say that I expect that all young people will openly listen to any unsolicited advice or even be interested in this subject matter. Often, we must go through self-discovery and our own process of making mistakes in order to seek out knowledge and guidance from others. But if I can stimulate some thought in any group of open minded youngsters or at least reach one young adult, then writing this book will have been entirely worth it. So, if you are an elderly person reading this book, I encourage you to distribute this book to any young adults in the process of starting their life path. If they understand these principles going forward, making future decisions perhaps will take on a different light. Understanding what constitutes health and happiness in life based on scientific and well-studied research can help reshape concepts of success.

Table of Contents

1. Dr. Nat Geo…………………………………………………………………Page 1
2. The Blue Zones Project……………………………………………….Page 11
3. Venturing Past the Blue Zone……………………………………Page 16
4. Blue Isn't the Only Color…………………………………………..Page 27
5. What is The Green Zone?...................................Page 29
6. The Basics of Getting Into The Green Zone………..Page 31
7. Advanced Green Zone Principles……………………………Page 57
8. Creating a Prescription Plan for Life…………………….Page 92
8. Appendix A………………………………………………………………Page 94
9. Appendix B………………………………………………………………Page 95
10. Appendix C………………………………………………………………Page 98
11. References………………………………………………………………Page 101

Dr. Nat Geo

Yes, I was surprised that I would start this book with a study that did not involve the National Institute of Health, CDC, World Health Organization or any one of the numerous Medical Organizations and Reputable Medical Journals I've become familiar with throughout the years. I find it amusing that my research led me to National Geographic. Oh I love those yellow borders that flash seemingly unreal photos at me and grab me so that I can't help but look inside and marvel at even more impossible wonders and cultures that could be alien for all I know from here sitting in my living room. Even my frequent international tours wouldn't venture to take me anywhere close to the likes of those far reaches of National Geographic. But this time, it was not Nat Geo who grabbed for my attention, but it was I who went searching for them. Why exactly did I start looking at a study that was conducted by National Geographic?

In brief, it wasn't any one thing, it was a series of nagging things. It was a combination of factors. Some of them included my family's obsession with different health diets, the constant dilemma of deciding my son's future with each spoonful of food, my interest in my own risk for diabetes based on a culture known for diabetic predilection, and my son's great-grandmother who even as I write presses on past 106 years old.

But go a little further back to what was just a gnawing feeling that started long before. It really began to stem from my growing discontent with my revolving hospital door practice. Patients coming in and out of the hospitals for chronic conditions and dependent on pain medications and never seeming to improve. I think I did better than most largely keeping my own patients out of the hospital, but it was a system-driven focus on making sure to take care of enough issues to keep them from getting worse and then getting them just well enough to go home. I did more in my office, but I constantly felt punished staying longer than most of the other office physicians because I generally spent more time talking with patients and examining them and creating detailed notes and plans. My patients complained that I never had appointments and I asked why they didn't go to one of the other multiple doctors in my practice since most of my work time was largely hospital related and I only kept part time office hours. But their answer was always that "You, Dr. George, actually care." And I say it here because it's true, I do care, probably too much. Yet during my training it was a constant issue, my caring. "You've got to learn to get out of the room". I was told over and over if I wanted to do well as a doctor, I needed to learn to be faster. Fifteen minutes was the magic number and "don't talk about more than 2 issues or you'll never be able to leave." Yet, something inside me just couldn't do that. Every time my patients said, I have another question, I remembered myself as a little girl with yet another bout of bronchitis, having waited 2, sometimes 3 weeks or if I was lucky enough to get an appointment the same day, sitting 2-3 hours in a waiting room choking down a nasty cough where a blind screen test would have pegged me as an 80 year old emphysema patient. And each time my hard-working parents would desperately pay out those copays just to put me in the hands of a doctor. So as a resident I felt an obligation to make sure there wasn't anything else the patient needed, or that they really understood their diagnosis or the treatment plan and usually there were endless diagnoses to sort through and tests to perform to determine if what was going on was this or that. Or because "oh, nobody ever told me the results of that test." And all of this had to be done by myself. I got faster, but still not enough to keep the 15 min rule. I suppose I could have gone into my own practice, but just think of the administrative work on top of everything else I was already doing. I felt wrong wanting to just spend time with my son and my family. It seemed to be a good doctor, I had to be the first one into the hospital and the last to leave, making sure to call my patients and follow up on all the tests even if it was 6 or 7pm and knowing that there was still paperwork waiting for me on my arrival home. I could never profess to know the truth, but I got the feeling that unfinished work didn't seem to bother other physicians as much. Somehow, for me though if I forgot to call someone back, I could barely sleep for fear of forgetting some important thing or the other, and they were all so important, believe me. I realized after thinking a little bit about it that while all doctors have the goal to take care of patients, hardly any of them knew what it meant to be a patient.

But not only did I know what that felt like, so did my husband who ultimately is my partner in crime, my best friend, but also my biggest teacher. Later he would become the hardest patient I would ever take care of, but also the one who would teach me the most. So in this book, at least in the beginning, I will talk a lot about him, because he is integral to the paradigm shift I had to go through to get to this point where I am now, teaching others about a new definition of health.

My husband's story started with chest pains shortly after immigrating to this country, ones that quickly morphed into headaches, then transformed into some degenerative disease that was waiting to be discovered. And then there it was, The Big C, Cancer. How do you tell someone nothing is wrong, when it is? And so we battled with the cancer and won! But it wasn't without its own casualties. The cancer attacked our relationship, the cancer attacked our trust in our bodies. Though we won the physical battle, the cancer had definitely beat us in the mental game. Soon, every pain had us wondering if the cancer was coming back. Every injury was not just a pulled muscle or aching joint, it was a metastasis. Every disagreement became tragic because arguing was such a waste of precious time. Headache, and it was time for a scan again, just to be sure. Yes, my husband got very much into his diet. I figured well, I myself didn't really drink or smoke, I didn't have any really bad habits, and I wasn't overweight, so I could pretty much eat whatever I wanted. But his theory was that his health started to go downhill when he left Mexico. He started to buy everything organic and with the birth of our son, diet became a battleground between the three of us from meats to vegetables to milk and treats, and as for my son, chicken nuggets were the solution of all. But, what was the real answer? It didn't help that Giselle at the same time publicly proclaimed that her kids ate vegetables like candy. Damn you Giselle for establishing yet another impossible female standard (but don't worry somehow we come to expect nothing less from fabulous Giselle). But what became even more apparent from this whole ordeal was that my husband had anxiety. And that anxiety was causing him to be hyper-focused on symptoms that the rest of us would just shrug off with a few seconds thought. And it wasn't just him, I too had developed anxiety over having to be a hard-edged doctor at work and soft and sweet mom at home and having to keep up my own façade that I too wasn't concerned about my husband having cancer. Ultimately all these things along with a multitude of other issues caused me to neglect myself in various ways. I suddenly found myself overweight, with severe back and neck pain, unable to sleep due to racing thoughts, and suddenly I was in a pit from which I couldn't find a way out. How could someone with a great job, living in beautiful Southern California, with everything one should have, feel she was at rock bottom?

This caused me to wonder about my patients. They didn't even have the resources I had and many struggled to cover the costs of the 10-25 essential pills which seemed to be commonplace amongst my patients above age 60. I tried with great difficulty to get rid of pills, but the hospital and medical guidelines made sure I knew that this patient should be on a b-blocker or lipid lowering med, or some ACE or anticoagulant and why with all the research was I not starting them all now? Because to me the sum of the parts didn't equal the whole. I knew they were great and proven and all the rage but somehow I couldn't believe that taking that much medicine all together every day could really be the right thing. Still I put my pen to my pad each day and tried to meet the standard of medical care as I tried to quash my guilt with double blind studies.

Paralleling my growing discomfort about my doctoral approach, I slowly began to realize that my own medical problems were related mostly to things outside my body, one of them being my husband's illness. And his illness was related to things he felt was out of his control such as my high intensity job, homesickness, and overwhelm at being a father. It began to really dawn on me in a new way that diabetes and obesity probably weren't just physical illnesses, but emotional illnesses for most people. I mean I already knew that in theory but I just didn't put it all together in full until I was under the mountain of it. Seems obvious doesn't it? Come on Dr. George, we all know that eating is stress related and that has to be emotional. Perhaps you could liken it to when you knew what the concept of love was, but until you first fell in love you didn't really get it in its entirety. I saw now the diabetic condition as an inability to keep in shape and control diet. But it wasn't just laziness or organic depression alone, it was an emotional pit that most people don't even know they are in. And some of them were not acutely aware they were depressed, they just accepted the pit they lived in with indifference. And what's more, it became socially acceptable to live in that pit, so they lacked the motivation to change. They lived with the same notion as my own parents had, in the meantime you go to the doctor when you are sick and do what they tell you, then you are doing the right thing. And even worse than all of that, I was giving my patients light bulbs to brighten their dark pits. And they thanked me for the cups of insulin I was lending them through the window of my very own dark pit of a hobble.

My epiphany led me to ask some rather unpleasant questions. Am I really helping my patients get healthier in the best way I can? Then something my wise husband told me years before in one of our not uncommon philosophical debates came back to me. I kept trying to dismiss it and I thought it extreme, but it rang a slight truth that seemed to hold on to me. He said, why would I listen to someone teach me to succeed in an area they have no real credentials in even if they claim to have experience. But now give me a person who has shown their own success in something, well that's someone who can tell me what to do next. I had always thought you could learn a little something from everyone, but I understood in some way he was right. It was way more efficient to go to someone who was already an expert to get instructions on how to do things right. When I started to think of how to beat the cancer, I started to think of who did beat cancer. Then I thought, why stop there? Why don't I go find out who has beaten it all and lived to tell the tale? That's when I became curious about the people that live the longest in the world.

Yes, I realized that my own patients were living longer, I had a handful of 90+ year old patients, but most were debilitated. But we are not talking about them, we are talking about the Millennials. These are the real Millennials, not the children of the baby boomers, these are the people who have the age to back the name.

That elite group, those Olympians of age that break the century barrier. They are the Michael Phelps of longevity. And I had direct access to one. My husband's grandmother. She was spitfire as we might say coming from the deep south. She was fairly functional, still walking and cooking, having logical conversations. Yeah, she had some issues, I mean she had dental problems. But I already had major dental problems in my early 20s. Yes, she was an elegant lady even while she was shooting spitballs at my husband at the restaurant table. She did this not because she was demented, she did it because she knew she had earned the right to get away with just about everything. And, of course we respected that right and allowed her to laugh at us as the spitballs came flying. And then I thought maybe it was genetics. Was it genetics? Several of her own kids had died of cancer. Maybe it wasn't just genetics. I thought back to my own traditional Indian culture and realized I didn't know a lot of adults in that community with cancer. Perhaps it was the diet; both she and my community still eats fresh cooked meals every day, made from scratch. Or even more plausible, must be those Mexican and Indian chili peppers I thought, caliente!

And, so with the thought of that elderly woman who still loved dolls in mind and with my husband's words still in the back of my mind, I went looking, looking to find the real experts. I mean I should be the expert, I did only go to school for 12 years to learn to take care of people's health. But somehow I don't recall that class about what actually helps people live longer. And let me be clear, none of this is to mean that surviving a heart attack isn't very important. But, instead of just laying down two more railroad tracks, why not find out who has already ridden the train there and back and ask them just how they have done it. Isn't that what they say, stand on the shoulders of giants, perhaps we won't actually do that to our millennials but we can apply the principle? Ok, so how has my grandmother-in-law outlived many of her own kids?

When I consulted Dr. Nat Geo, my eyes opened to a world I never would have imagined. Why hadn't this been researched by the National Institutes of Health or anyone in the health field? I mean our goal isn't just to survive a heart attack, is it? Isn't it to survive and live a long life? But, ultimately, I am glad someone asked the question and created this endeavor to answer it. And though it did not originate from medical professionals, it was funded by the people who most benefit from us living longer, none other than our beloved insurance companies. I was extremely fascinated. Dan Buettner and his blue zones team (Buettner, The Blue Zones: Lessons for Living Longer From the People Who've Lived the Longest, 2008), *they* had the right idea. Let's not just interview a few Millennials and see what they are doing, let's find as many as we can and find out what they are all doing. And that's exactly what they did. They employed medical researchers and epidemiologists to tediously work through mass piles of data on these people. And guess what, they found out that there were physical hot spots and locations of people living over 100. Sounds like something out of X-files. And then the team set out to establish the commonalities between these specific groups who generally outlived the rest of society. They dissected out from all the raw data overlaps that existed between the different communities such as in the diagram here.

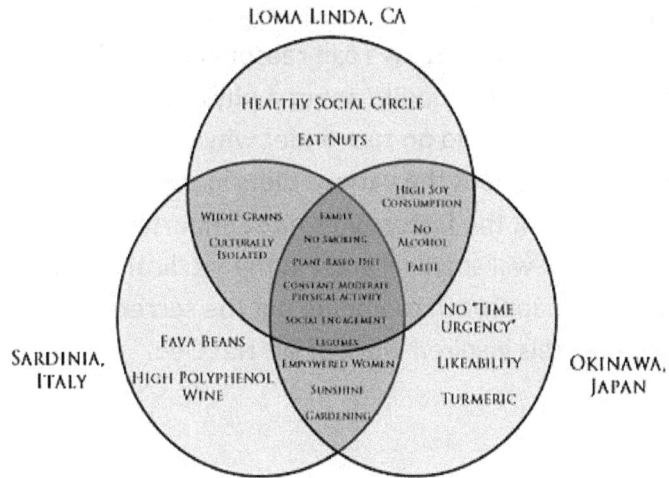

Using these overlaps, they homed in on the factors that must be contributory directly or indirectly to longevity. They mapped a guideline for others to follow as a formula for longevity. As the summer of my epiphany rolled on, I got other signs that perhaps formulas for success are not as far-fetched as one might believe. I mean, how does the Jamaican track team dominate that field? How did the Karolyis dominate gymnastics in two different countries? People had found the formula for success in their areas and demonstrated them visibly for the rest of us.

Why not learn from these, our giants and experts, our gold medalists on health? In these blue zone communities, you have uniquely different identifiable strengths. Besides outliving the rest of the population, each seems to have its own niche claim to fame. One group has the longest living women in the world. Another group has the longest living men. One group exhibited very low levels of dementia. Another group has extremely low rates of disability and the last group is nestled right in the midst of the modern western world. So, we can reasonably say that it isn't just genetics or some sort of oddity about a physical locale. I found this all fascinating.   Now I go on to wonder why we aren't doing controlled studies about the various diets in all these communities to find out which of the factors was most important. I hope perhaps my book will spark interest in the medical community to take a back-step approach to finding out the secrets of longevity and continuing this inspired work of Dr. Nat Geo.

The Blue Zones Project

So, Dr. Nat Geo identified 5 zones or communities where people outlived at a higher rate the rest of the world's population. These include the following locales (Buettner, 2008). In these locales, the average person lives to age 90 and often past age 100, whereas the rest of society on average only lives to age of 78 years old. Here are the specific locations where this phenomenon was found to occur. Amazingly, these communities are spread out across the world and yet all seem to know some secret the rest of us don't.

> Loma Linda, CA
>
> Okinawa, Japan (yes that's the one in Karate Kid)
>
> Nicoya, Costa Rica
>
> Sardinia, Italy
>
> Ikaria, Greece.

Now, in the next few sections, we'll review in brief the factors that Buettner and his team identified. My goal is not to rehash what Buettner and his team already revealed to us some years ago, but to provoke discussion on these factors and integrate them into a plan for living not only long lives, but happy ones as well.

When I reviewed the findings of the blue zones project (1), what I found interesting was that the critical factors that were highlighted as integral to longevity did not include taking an aspirin daily or that everyone went to their doctor every year. The relevant factors were not about getting early cancer screenings or having the best access to healthcare facilities. In fact, the only attributable factor that was related to a medicinal type intervention was a moderate alcohol intake. Was I surprised? Well of course. And yes, I still believe in medications and surgery and the treatments I have been trained in. I don't think people would live so long without antibiotics and appendectomies and our Western medical standard. It just means that I realize as a bigger picture overall health is likely very greatly influenced by those factors identified in the Blue Zones research and as with my husband and myself, there are other extracorporeal (non-physical) factors that must be considered as well. This is what I hope to teach in detail, an understanding of these factors and more which we will go into later in the next few chapters. And diet, yes I had wanted to ignore that diet was important as long as you were not overweight. But the Blue Zones Project really hammered home a confirmation that dietary considerations are important.

Ultimately the Blue Zones Project inspired me to start looking at end-goals for myself, my family and my patients. But it also sparked my curiosity about some other new questions. Thanks again Dr. Nat Geo!

Blue Zone Concepts

a. Do not overeat.

The rule of 80% percent full seems to apply here. The Millennials take their time in eating so that they do not overeat as a rule.

b. Moderate exercise is best.

No extreme fitness programs here. Millennials exercise daily, moderately and as a part of their daily activities and functions. Walking is a big part of this exercise regimen.

c. Social Relationships are key

Supportive relationships and lifelong friendships are important, very important to the health of the Millennial society.

d. Gardening

Outdoor activities, specifically Gardening seems to help with longevity.

e. Finding a Purpose or Passion in Life

Having a Purpose or Passion in life is key to prolonging one's subconscious will to live and survive.

f. Moderate Alcohol Intake.

While not every Blue Zone Community drinks, most of them have moderate alcohol intake in social settings.

g. Plant Based or Vegetarian Fresh Diets

Most of the Blue Zone Communities are not heavily focused on meat and protein intake, although protein does compose a small portion of the diet, fresh cooked food mainly vegetables tend to be central to the Millennial diet

h. Spiritual or Religious activities.

Most Blue Zoners engage in once weekly structured Religious activities.

i. Tea

Tea, more specifically Green Tea seems to be a common intake amongst Blue Zoners. They drink tea as often as 4-5 x/day.

j. Stress Reduction

Blue Zoners spend considerable time and place priority on stress reducing activities and habits.

k. Positive Outlook on Life

Positivity is king in the world of the Blue Zoner.

I. Living in a Society that promotes health will promote an individual's health

J. Marriage and family is the number one priority within blue zone societies.

These references can be found in Dan Buettner's book or on the Blue Zones Website (1).

Venturing Past the Blue Zone

Spy vs Spy vs Spy

Health is a very complicated word.

My husband was and is one of the healthiest people I know. Imagine if you took a person who had never driven a car before and asked them out of the blue not only to drive for the first time, but to drive in a snowstorm even having perfect vision and great reflexes. Now ask a person who had driven 20 years in the rain and light snow flurries to do the same even though they needed glasses and drove slower due to delayed reflexes. Which do you suppose would do better? Tough choice isn't it, much like our last political election. My opinion, is that our ability to handle various situations isn't always dependent only on our physical abilities. Most often it is related to our experience and exposure. That is why I initially found it odd that my husband, in peak condition with vague symptoms should lose more sleep over his health than any of my patients with their 25 different comorbid conditions and the multitude of pills they took daily to maintain that semi-sweet state of health they had come to subsist on.

I started to understand that, actually, I was treating two different groups of patients. One type was like my husband. And I saw it clearly. It usually was a young to middle age person who was in peak condition, no medications and no conditions. But suddenly they were in the doctor's office for something. It might have been in reality something small or something major, but either way, the reaction was the same. There was a certain look of shock and fear that was on the face. A slight tremble was apparent in the movements and uncertainty at what was next. You could generally find a slight sheen of sweat appear when any waiting for tests or if results were involved.

And then there was my other group of patients. We lovingly in my doctoral residency called them the ones with "bad plasma". Many of them had rheumatologic diseases or immune disorders. Some were young or others were my elderly patients that had survived 3 different types of cancers and had rotator cuff injuries and multiple other conditions just to ice the cake. But these were the confident ones, the ones that explained calmly that their pain was managed by so and so, and this is how they treated their MS flares. There was no sweating, no trembling, no downturn in the body posture when we said tests needed to be done.

I realized then that health was much like an exercise. You couldn't just up and run the biggest race of your life without any preparation much as it was in any sport. To expect that would be like asking a baby to go mountain hiking after demanding he change his own very first diaper. Who was truly healthier? Was it my patients that had never had any medical conditions or the ones who didn't seem to be phased by anything and kept trekking along, illness after illness? And even more important seemed to be how I phrased what would happen. If I prepared my patients for the worst, they were able to handle it. The mental preparation was very important. The expectation was extremely important. And the sicker they had been during their life before these moments of critical illness the better they were at focusing on their treatments than the depravity of the illness itself.

But there was also a problem with that too. While my "peak performers" had an extreme view of health that was shattered by any small insult to their health, my "poor plasma" patients also had their own problematic twisted view of health. These patients that kept battling through illnesses over and over, they had somehow settled comfortably on a standard of health where they never expected to be well. That was my problem before too. Perhaps that is why I focused so much on other things rather than exercise or fitness or beauty, because I never expected that those things were for me and I settled into a standard of chronically being ill.

These two extreme models of patient perspective remind me of that old political cartoon Spy vs Spy. This is a cartoon where two rats keep trying to outwit each other. The comedy is you know that both are stuck in their own clearly warped views of reality and neither will win. And to you and me it's obvious that they simply need to step away from their subversive cycle of warfare to end their own pain. But only some of you may recall there was for a time a 3rd spy. I relate to her. She was the Grey Spy and she usually won by utilizing the extreme obsessions of the other two to her advantage. But I wasn't always a Grey Spy, I started out as of those other poor rats. I was a "poor plasma" patient myself.

What changed me from being the chronically ill person to what I am now? What got me out of my own rat race was discovering ways to address my health problems in ways that this medical system had failed me on. And helping me with that was at the same time, watching my husband do the same with his health problems.

Lizard Legs Goes to the Dentist and Sneezes up a Lung

Let's talk about me first and spare my husband a little while longer.

When I was young I had several annoying health issues. One was extremely dry skin on my legs. The second was that I had dental cavities that were disproportionate for my age. I had bad environmental allergies so that I couldn't venture outdoors much. And I developed recurrent bouts of severe bronchitis at least 3-4 x per year.

Skin is a big issue for a kid and it was for me too. It's no fun being called lizard legs. Thankfully I didn't have the eczema that my grandfather had. But usually, I was told I didn't drink enough water, and those looks of disdain really got me feeling self-conscious at an early age. I thanked my lucky stars that I ended up at a school that didn't allow anyone to wear shorts and I dreaded gym. I spent most of high school visiting various dermatologists, who recommended expensive prescriptions creams, steroids, and other remedies none of which worked. Let's see, frigidly cold showers, wearing wraps at night with Vaseline. The best was using Crisco though. I felt like buttered bread most of the time.

At the same time of my life, much to my bewilderment, I had cavity after cavity. Granted I wasn't great at taking care of my teeth. But what kid flosses every single day? I had cavity after cavity after cavity meanwhile watching my brother who ate similarly to me never have a cavity. Boy, I sure dreaded death at the hands of my old dentist who didn't seem to think I needed to breathe much and generally let me choke on my own spit. Yet another condition with an awful stigma. It wasn't until years later I identified how this was not even close to my fault. But between the constant speeches of how it had to be my poor hygiene that was at fault or my mom's theory that my distaste for milk was the driving factor undermining any other valid beliefs out there, essentially, I reasoned that my suffering was my own fault.

As if that wasn't enough for a kid. See, this is where I think I held on loosely to the fact that something about all of this was largely out of my doing. Bronchitis. They said I had childhood asthma. Lucky for me, they did already know about this triad of atopic dermatitis, with the skin problems, bronchitis, and allergies. It subconsciously must have registered that if this was a known conglomerate of illnesses, that it somehow had nothing to do with what I was doing or had done. They didn't say at the time that it was a genetic condition, but it was a known constellate of conditions that existed even between different races and societies. So, when people told me about my own culpability, somehow, I managed to only just shrug them off and keep my dignity that it wasn't my own fault that I was the way I was. And the added confirmation of that was that my mom was similar. She wasn't quite as bad, but she had the same constellation of symptoms as I did.

Nevertheless, I still had to deal with these things. Coexisting with my bronchitis were severe allergies. I was a tomboy and loved to run and play and be physical. I loved the outdoors, I just wasn't allowed to go to that club. I watched from the windows as other kids played without a care in the world. I traveled with my tissue paper wad friend everywhere and we stayed out of the grass as much as possible, knowing that a romp in the grass would end up with and uncontrollable sneezing frenzy. When I wanted to go on our musical exchange to Japan, I raised money by cutting grass for people. My dad sat by in the car watching as I was determined and stubborn, but he insisted I wear a mask. It was odd to see a little Indian girl in a hospital mask pushing around a lawnmower in 100 degree weather wearing full length pants.

So, I guess I was a pretty odd little kid, but I didn't feel that way. I felt just fine, and as I said, I accepted most of my dysfunction. It wasn't until college that I could no longer accept being lizard legs. I had grown into a spindly teenager. I saw other girls wearing their cute skirts and short dresses and the heat was near unbearable in the South. Athens, Georgia was a place you just couldn't hate and so I fell in love with it. It was a great place to be. The reason I am bringing this up is because suddenly I did have a motivation to change. I wanted to fit in like other girls. I wanted not to be an odd man out before I even opened my mouth. This motivation was very important. We'll talk about that more later. Don't worry, poor plasma rarely goes anywhere.

Now let's talk about my husband.

He was briefly a Dolce & Gabbana model. I had never met someone with such a perfect physique in real life. I mean, I guess the celebrities were like that, but that was behind the glow of the cameras and makeup and with the help of expensive trainers and special diets. But in real life, I had never met anyone so healthy. Yes, I was attracted to that perfect physique. But I swear there were other things too! Perhaps I was attracted to his physique but not in the way you would imagine, but in a way of being awe-inspired by his careless health. There was no effort in his perfect health. He just was. And I was drawn to that ability just as a nerdy little kid was drawn to the popular kids. I was drawn to that skill, for it must have been a skill to be that perfect in physique and in health. So, join me for a second as I was before and let's willingly or unwillingly focus on this perfect physique. My future husband at that time, hadn't a clue about what flossing was, though he generally brushed his teeth but came out with clean bill from his dental check. He ate 3x the normal person's diet without a single ounce of fat deposited on his body. He had perfect skin and never really put on lotion or had any other such skin care regimen. He played soccer and basketball as many active young boys did. He said he was just as tall as his friends, but at 6'2", he loomed over most Mexicans. Before we were married I had never so much as seen him have a cold. It was pretty incredible.

Yes, he was a picture of health; that is until he came to the U.S. after we were married. You already know a bit of the story, the pains and the cancer, but when it rains it pours. Within a year of the cancer, my husband was also diagnosed with acid reflux and bilateral arthritis of the knees. His hairline started receding even in his late 20s and he began with sinus issues that would plague him for over a year. Now of course I realize he was the type of patient that couldn't handle that decathlon of disease. He had barely had a cold in the 8 years of our relationship prior to that time. But this is not something I would understand until much later. To me, being ill was second nature. My reassurances to him that he was still in better shape than anyone I knew passed over his worried mind without providing any real comfort.

Time to Reset

As I read about The Blue Zoners and their approach to keeping their bodies in shape and in the same time that my husband was diagnosed with rather severe arthritis for his age it caused me to understand the body in a different way. I had always thought of the body as this magic, can- do everything little engine if you kept-it-in-shape kind of model. Mind over matter was real to me. And the evidence to that were the old people who could still dance. But now I saw it differently, the body was truly affected by the way we viewed it. I guess I had learned in medical school all about the problems that the human body could face, but we had only discussed few of its actual limitations. My society praised physical feats of strength and extreme fitness. You see it everywhere, 0% fat bodies, no carb diets. Again, this reframed my thought process of the origination of physical ailments and what leads me now to approach patients, using this, my new perspective. I started again to understand something that I had known all along in a deeper way that was more crucial. The Blue Zoners practiced moderation in seemingly everything. And that was what it was more than just the diet or the specific individual practices or commonalities. My theory is that Blue Zoners don't topple because they are balanced. They didn't do extreme. They didn't eat extreme, they didn't exercise extreme, they didn't allow emotional extremes. The only extreme I felt they did practice perhaps was extreme positivity and maybe they even didn't shun occasional bouts of negativity, my guess is that it is acceptable for them to share those moments.

As I looked back at my own life to see what I did that could be in keeping with The Blue Zoners, there wasn't much of a relation. I didn't eat like them. I didn't exercise the same way. But there was one thing we had in common. I was a social creature. Or rather, I had learned to be a social creature. As a youth I was very shy, but I had very good friends be it two or three. I eventually lost most of my shyness and friendships came naturally to me. I thought back to my childhood and all of the things that I had gone through. How had I managed my own problems? I realized it was because I was social. I had balanced my stress by sharing it with others. I no longer had to deal with it alone. The burden was so much lighter. I didn't know it at the time, but I was practicing one of the principles that Blue Zoners often engage in. It is a principle that the Nat Geo team would refer to as a stress reducing exercise. But I call it offloading as I learned of it in a different context while I was learning about music therapy (24).

Regardless of how I had learned this tool, my train of thought took me to how offloading had often helped me to handle extreme stress. I thought of how offloading was like a table. If you tried to put all the stress onto one leg, the table would surely not be able to stand. But with 4 legs or even just 3 legs, a table could hold an enormous amount of weight. But the weight had to be distributed evenly. And it was then that it hit me. Balance was the key. Perhaps the Chinese have known this for years, Ying and Yang and all that. Buddha was definitely a proponent for it. But why did I feel like the true message of that was lost on us during modern times? If that was the key, why then does our society place emphasis on our career success so much over all the other things? Why do kids not learn balance in school or other principles of stress management? This is when I realized I had to do a reset in my own life. I couldn't just see my career success as life success. And it didn't equate anyway. Being at the top of my field didn't seem to bring me more happiness. It just forced me to ask what I really wanted the rest of my days to look like. That was a good point to be at, because I realized I had something more important to do other than pushing prescriptions, so that I could help the world. I had to help others reset their lives as well.

I never intended on being any sort of life coach. I mean even if I hadn't already done 12 years of higher level school, if I had wanted to specialize, it should have been rather intuitive to specialize in a traditional field like Dermatology or GI or Allergy/Immunology. But the conundrum of how I was now healthier than my husband, even with lizard legs and coughing up a lung brought me full circle as to what my definition of health was. I like to think of myself as a health strategist. I deduced that my husband's medical problems were related predominantly to his stress and anxiety. I'm almost positive he somehow unwittingly manifested his own cancer, though I don't currently have a way to prove it. But there does exist real data supporting that high levels of stress directly or indirectly increase inflammatory markers in the body and may be related to the cellular agents that are causative of many cancer processes.

This topic is still under much debate, but several sources are supporting this theory. As for myself, my health personally started to crumble as my husband's health issues did not resolve. My stress also manifested physically and created a cycle of bad habits. What was odder to me is that my husband was getting treatment for his cancer, yet I wasn't being treated at all even when I too suffering from cancer. It was only after I actively recognized my own need for help and sought it out on my own that I began to piece all these seemingly unrelated things together into one picture.

I then realized that it was not enough to just treat the body's physical ailments. I wasn't entirely sure how, but I knew I had to help people to not only survive, not only be in physically good shape, but to treat their health; as a whole. That meant investigating all their problems. They were not independent of each other. They were very much related. It brought me back to when I was a resident in the intensive care unit. I hadn't a clue at the time what I was doing being a student. But as they taught me to do, I learned to list out all the problems and create a plan for each one. I slowly realized that it was just as important to treat all the little problems for the patient to do well. It was easy to overlook or ignore small issues or seemingly unrelated issues. But that was only because the human mind and body are so complex, and we still are not clear on how everything is related. I quickly learned that those small things suddenly could become crucial and that you could prevent a major complication by treating a small problem early. Yes, I am now in a position of highly integrating many experiences and thought processes from throughout my life and work. It is incredible when you finally undergo a paradigm shift. I decided I needed to go beyond the Blue Zone. I needed to find out how to live well, not just live. It is like seeing the world in black and white and then experiencing it in color, just as you might recall that scene from The Wizard of Oz. And if you can't tell, I do so love movies and television.

Blue Isn't the Only Color

Changing my perspective to look at what people were doing right instead of what they were doing wrong, gave me a new curiosity. Much as I had asked myself, if surviving was enough, I started to wonder if living was the only end-goal. Yes, here were the Blue Zoners. They knew how to live long lives. But is that the only point? Why was I thinking that? My now infamous grandmother-in-law (Abuelita) as we call her, was trudging along, fully functional. But my conversations about how she was doing inevitably ended with her being depressed. I mean who wouldn't be? When you are 106 every bedtime has to be rather frightening. And outliving yet another child must make you feel so guilty and sad. So is it really enough to just live longer? I started to wonder about the other color. I wanted to know about state of Yellow or the Yellow Zone as I call it. Would you be my sunshine? Yes, yellow is the universal color of happiness. I said to myself even if I did learn the secrets to living a long life, do I really want to live that long if I'm not happy? At least for me, the answer is no. I want to live long and happy if I can. I imagined that state as being in a room full of sunshine. A place of safety and warmth and joy. This is the Yellow Zone. And I want the same for everyone. The Yellow Zone as it were, is not a large-scale project funded by our insurance companies and National Geographic. But that doesn't mean there aren't people out there that are curious about this very subject.

So now I began another search for information and data. This time it was for the secrets to happiness. And surprisingly there have been studies on this as well, though not as expansive and comprehensive as Nat Geo's endeavor. Many small groups have ventured to identify the keys to this state of being. And Harvard recently has put out results on a 75-year study on the topic. This is a very important publication, but as I researched more, I looked for other things, places where people were generally happier in the same manner as Nat Geo had done came up with a list of factors from various science-based research and articles. I utilized this to figure what I could do to improve my own happiness. My way of thinking about things shifted yet again. Now I had the formula. I didn't only just have the formula of how to live a long life. Now I also had the formula to live a happy life. It was a choice. I often told my son that he could choose to be happy or sad. But I suppose I had to choose also. This is what I choose. I don't choose more money or to be 0% body fat. I am no longer concerned about my performance day to day. I now am only concerned in engaging in behaviors I know will enhance my overall goals of health and happiness. This took the pressure off each little thing I did. I knew that when you have the formula to something, that if you just followed the steps, you would get to what you were after.

Once I realized this for myself though, it hit me again. Other people don't have the formula. That is the only reason they cannot achieve the same goals. I began to see patterns everywhere. Like why the Williams sisters are both at the top of the Tennis game. Or how the Manning brothers dominate the football stadiums. Or how a songwriter can often write 100 hits while the rest of us would dream of writing just one. Or even why it seems easy for Indian people to get into and through medical school. They know the formula and they also carry it out step by step. It's not a secret. It's only a secret to our eyes alone. So, I felt that after acquiring this precious information and knowledge, I must go on to share these concepts with anyone who has a desire to learn.

What is the Green Zone?

A green room in historical and popular culture is a room where celebrities wait for a TV or stage performance. It is their private space to do whatever they need to get ready for their live performances. It could involve getting dressed, practicing lines, putting on makeup, or getting into character. Historically, these rooms were lined with a material called green baize that acted as soundproofing so that artists could practice their lines without fear (4). But often artists report this is where they were able to get into the right frame of mind to do their job.

In less popular culture, the green room is a surfing term (5). Only a handful of hardcore surfers have entered the green room, which is when a surfer catches a wave and in a perfect mastery of the sport are able to ride the wave even until the wave folds over onto itself. This creates a barrel within the wave, and if you are lucky enough to be able to experience this, you will find yourself enclosed within a "room" with walls of green. Surfers report this as a zone of ultimate Zen. They say it is the one of the most peaceful and serene settings. This excerpt from a surfing article may explain it best. "If you understand the wave and how it moves, you don't have to be afraid of it (or at the very least, you can be less afraid). After all, when you break a wave down to its basic nature, it is just cycling energy moving through water. When the conditions are right, when the water is shallow enough, the wave is born. When I realized this on an experiential level, the waves lost their ability to paralyze me. I began to see through them and enjoy riding them.... And when a beautiful wave comes... we can catch it, maybe even get inside the hollow tube and see its beautiful emptiness (6)."

I found this concept fascinating, because of so many factors.

First, it is something that few people will experience. Why is that? The truth is, like many rare experiences, it takes a mastery and skill that few people dedicate themselves to. The commitment required is high, but to those who have experienced it, it is worth it. It also takes a mental fortitude to get past failure, to continually try to improve and it requires a harmony and trust with the universe and nature. Additionally, people who do get into the Green Room or Green Zone, they must have a higher understanding of how the universe works but they are able to trust in the rules of that universe. Lastly, they somehow simultaneously must give up control over their environment, but, yet they demonstrate a masterful control of the experience. And, as an added bonus, the color green represents our trend to be more eco-friendly and eco-healthy with ourselves and our world.

I think this demonstration and these definitions work perfectly as to combining the Blue Zones concepts with the Yellow Zone concepts giving us an understanding of how to enter The Green Zone, the place of ultimate Zen. Combining basic principles like combining the primary colors can give us a new color, a new perspective on life. I want to reiterate that all the data I present here is not just my own opinion but is based on scientific research and focused studies as listed in References.

Learn the Basics of Getting into The Green Zone

It's All About Relationships

What I learned from studying both the Blue Zoners and Happiness Research is what I will dissect here for you. The number one factor crossing between both these lines of research were relationships. This proves yet again, we were designed to be social creatures. Harvard's study took 75 years to reveal what is the single most important factor that contributes to happiness, and that is relationships (3).

Relationships seem to be central to both happiness and longevity. But to be more precise, not just any relationships, and not just how many friends you have on Facebook. The relationships must be warm and supportive. Blue Zoners put emphasis on retaining proximity to extended family, but it took me quite some time to evaluate this and in deciphering happiness and longevity studies, this may not be applicable if your family is toxic. Those type of relationships are not encouraged. If you do have toxic familial relationships, you may be able to create the supportive network you need outside of your family if you are for other reasons unable to maintain relationships within your biological family, due to the fact that they are unhealthy. The focus should be on warm, supportive, encouraging relationships of quality and not quantity. This applies also to marriage. Supportive and healthy marriages are especially important. While many people supposed I had intended this book for a geriatric audience, I really believe young people are the ones who will most benefit from the principles in this book. Therefore, I am encouraging my young readers to consider this as a factor when thinking of life paths and choices. If you are considering a move for work or school, consider how this might affect your long-term goals. I personally understood this better only after I had a child. I didn't understand as a youth myself that moving for school or work sets into motion a cascade of events that ground and root you into a particular locale. Later I found that practically and emotionally it was difficult being away from my family, though I had a good life in the city I lived in. Mainly this was because I realized that my son wouldn't be able to share those experiences with his grandparents at whim. In addition, childrearing is difficult on your own, with no help. Family support with childcare provides a disproportionate relief to young parents. A few hours break while aunts and uncles or grandparents take over can restore energy and patience to exhausted parents. Knowing that you have backup and support in emergency situations also can reduce stress levels. Also, that extended family structure creates a strong sense of identity and place to a child. That foundation appears to be critical to lifelong happiness and fortitude in dealing with problems for the child and for aging family members. But again, if you can't have access to this family structure due to physical barriers or unhealthy family structures do your best to create one where you are.

Perspective Changes Everything

It couldn't be as simple as just relationships, could it? I had many good relationships. I didn't always feel like I was the happiest person though. I believed this research was accurate and yet, I thought there must be something more involved in creating happiness. It must be as it was for the Blue Zone research more of the bigger picture than just one single factor. The next seemingly important factor that crossed between the principles of happiness and longevity was a matter of perspective. Glass-full people tend to have better results than glass half empty people. Genetics and young experience plays a part in whether you are one versus the other. But overwhelming positivity seems to be key in maintaining a long and happy life (7). So, I must promote that if you are not a person born with a positive outlook on life, then undertake exercises to change (that is if you would like to get into The Green Zone, otherwise just stay Green like the Grinch!) Contrary to popular belief, you can change this if you want to. It may be harder for some people than others, but it is entirely possible and achievable. There are numerous techniques. If you are not sure which type of person you are, then consider if you tend to be pessimistic, that generally has a relation with having a negative outlook on life and a low level of self-worth. There is no shame in it, although if you are pessimistic you are probably doubting that statement presently. I personally know that somewhere in my past I was able to change that in myself. One of the main exercises that you can engage in is with positive affirmations. These are repeated statements that oppose and battle the negative ideas that pop into your head. Also, instrumental in metamorphosis is again, eliminating toxic relationships that are present in your life and surrounding yourself with people who believe in you and encourage you and act as healthy role models which will contribute to you having and developing a more positive outlook.

As an illustration, there are great examples of how important perspective can be. One is a story of an old woman who spent a few hours every week cleaning the shells of turtles from the algae and dirt that accumulated on their shells. A passerby states that most turtles spend their lives similarly with dirt and algae on their shells and with no one to help them. She agrees, and the passerby says that her efforts affect probably less than 1% of the turtles in the world, so wouldn't her time be better spent doing something else. They ask how exactly these efforts were making a difference. She wisely responds, "If this little turtle could talk, he'd tell you I made all the difference in the world." Another movie reference is *Life is Beautiful* which takes this concept to an extreme; but is a perfect illustration of how perspective is so important. At the end of this book I will include a list of movies and/or books that really impact conceptual perspectives of life.

Another topic I am fascinated by is how to affect perspective. When I started working out with my trainer, I explained to him I wasn't bred in a culture of fitness and activity. So I asked him how he kept going and seemed to enjoy working out. He implied, it isn't that it is less painful, it is just that his vision of what he was achieving kept him excited for what was doing. So he focused on what he was getting out of it, on the vision of the body he wanted, not on how the workouts felt. I realized, this is also true for people who have difficulties in work environments. They may argue and struggle with having to stay a few minutes later or about certain injustices that happen in their place of work. Other people thrive because they focus on the bigger picture. They may understand that by creating lots of noise about little things is exactly what business owners do not want to deal with, so they let little things slide. You may say that is entirely ridiculous to allow yourself to be taken advantage of, but I have observed that the most successful people don't dwell on those little things and are often given the highest promotions and salary increases and with time they have more control over their work environment and on improving those unjust and unfair or inefficient practices. That is not to say let yourself be abused, but if it is a matter of a few small things here and there, don't lose it. Or if you are not getting to work on time, think of it from a different perspective like that of the business owner who has hired you to help them keep their business successful. Would you want to deal with an employee who was consistently late even if it was just a few minutes? Your goal should not be to just to do your job, but to do what helps your company. Understanding the bigger picture means you will see how best to become essential to your company and how your company and colleagues can tremendously benefit from your presence simply by employing your positive perspective. So, keeping an eye on the bigger prize and long-term goals helps smooths out the tiny aches and pains of day to day life. In fact, many positive minded people tend to look back on those small frustrations with fondness later in life akin to a friendly frat hazing.

Positive minded people also react to mistakes and failures differently than the other side. They see it as an expected part of the process. So, when it happens, they are not surprised. They also try to learn from those things to prevent them from happening again down the road. Negative minded people usually have unrealistic goals of perfection so when something goes wrong, they cannot handle it and many times even give up.

Positivity releases endorphins that allow people to continue even with frustration and setbacks. Though I didn't list it is a main factor above, it was established that Blue Zoners also seemed to laugh a lot and sing and hum. These activities improve their mood and positive outlook on life.

So, my recommendation is to watch some comedy specials, do some karaoke which will increase singing *and* laughing, and try to consider other more positive possibilities if the first idea that comes to mind is a negative possibility. I especially encourage this for people who feel that others are always attacking or criticizing them. Yes, sometimes there are mean people, but most people are just looking for acceptance. If someone says something off color, think of what they might have been trying to say or what their intention was. Try to hear the underlying intention, not the specific words. This will help you avoid anxiety and conflict with other people.

Stress Reduction

While having a positive outlook on life automatically reduces stress, it is important to emphasize also active stress reduction techniques (9). The happiest people in the world know how to proactively unplug and unwind. It is amazing how stress can impact life. We each manifest it differently. In the medical field, it is well known that stress increases risks for heart attack. (Lancet, 8). But from my own observation and some supporting studies, I truly believe that we manifest stress in so many ways. Anxiety and panic attacks, back pain, numbness and neurologic conditions, sleep disturbances, eating disorders, viral outbreaks (such as herpes), and even cancer. I am surprised we don't give more emphasis to stress reduction in our society. Asia, I think does give some importance to this, thus their thriving industries of chiropractic, acupuncture, and massage services, as well as focus on meditation, yoga, and tai chi.

Unfortunately, Western society places little emphasis on this currently. In fact, we often glorify high stress positions and activities in our society. I hope we can change this for the sake of our well-being. I have been reading a lot about business leaders and executives who run companies that are valued at a billion dollars, and they are on the covers of magazines all the time, and we praise the 80+plus hour work weeks that are their lives. For some this may be the ideal life, but I do believe we must reconsider our definitions of wealth and success. Because I don't know that this really could be the life we want to promote to our kids. I won't say that as a catch-all because each situation is different but if we praise that dedication over commitment to child-rearing, then we have definitely gotten things wrong.

I really want to talk about what is going on in society today. Mass shootings have become a sort of a public complaint box in this country. My husband and I talk about it all the time, what is the point of this action? Why do people feel the need to go out and lead a mass shooting? What we can only gather from speculation is that those individuals did not get the foundation and acceptance they needed as a child. They did not have support or validation in their youth. What we forget about with 80-hour work weeks is that somewhere something is being neglected. As a medical student and resident which was an 80+ hour week (in fact before my time it used to be closer to 100 hrs+), I neglected cleaning and cooking and exercising. I often wondered how the gatekeepers of health could live so unhealthy. We didn't sleep for 36 hours at a stretch. Often during work, I wouldn't drink water, so I wouldn't need to go to the bathroom during a surgery or when I was very busy, and I pondered several times if I would qualify for renal insufficiency based on my bad habits. So somewhere, something *has to* suffer. I wonder if the suffering may not be as we think a direct consequence, but indirectly how we now must deal with a generation of latchkey kids who never saw their parents though they had comfortable lives. Yet those comforts didn't provide the true needs of the children. I feel my own counterparts are becoming more aware of this. Many families are choosing to be one-income households so a parent (mom or dad) is always at home and kids have that foundation that truly only their own parents can provide. Also, I don't know that we are perfect by any means, but this generation of parents has become highly conscious of how their actions affect their children. I am witnessing change in people which is rapid and amazing in so many family related issues from learning about healthy diets, mastering communication, learning about healthy types of discipline and trying to understand the real needs of children. We have already seen companies that have adopted progressive and yet productive styles of work such as Google and Facebook, who promote relaxation and creativity to move their businesses ahead over a punch clock style of work. Our society is trending towards working smarter, not harder, which I think is fabulous.

So, in this section, I promote taking care of yourself through stress reducing activities. Consider the following activities to help you achieve this. Massage, also chiropractic or acupuncture, yoga, meditation, journaling, having a support group (Okinawans all do this). Other less thought of activities includes owning a pet (12), (remember they do need a lot of attention though), coloring and artwork, and doing community services. These should be a part of a preventative routine and not just for when you feel stress is getting out of your control. I also want you to consider what specific events trigger you to have stress. For example, I do not like being late, so I purposefully forward my clocks so that I am generally able to be on time (If I ever show up late, I promise you it bothers me more than it does you). I want you to also consider factors for a spouse or significant other, that can promote arguments or stress in them which feeds back to ourselves. If you know there is something you can do or avoid or alter to help their stress levels, then you can improve both of your quality of life. Really sit down together and learn what causes stress for each other and what brings you both comfort and relaxation. Sometimes it's not as difficult as you may believe.

Faith Based Activities

So, you don't believe in God, well just act like it! (10) Look, I have always known that someone has been taking care of me and call that someone what name you will. In medical school while learning about the body, I was astounded at the system that is behind the workings of the human body. I could not feign anything less than amazement. The body was designed as was an Italian racecar. We are not even yet sophisticated enough to understand completely how it works. My opinion, is that it could not exist without enormous thought having gone into it. Perhaps only medical professionals can gather what I mean. But if you don't believe in God or Divinity, that is okay. I am not asking you to. What I will promote here is that you start to engage in relationships with other people or if you are comfortable, even better in a faith-based community. Most people who live long and happy lives, *as per research,* engage in Faith based activities. What I have found is in the beginning you may not understand how it works or believe in the process. But I want you to recall when you were learning to ride a bicycle or learning to swim. Most of us as children were truly afraid or didn't believe that those processes were real or reliable. Most of us *knew* we would fall or that we would sink and drown. What happened in actuality though is that we had someone telling us that it was possible, that we could ride a bike, that we could float and that person was someone who knew the mechanics or the steps to make it happen. Momentarily we might have a setback but then it clicked. Yes, in the beginning we never believe. We as humans believe when we ourselves live the experience. So, I am working on a way to help people through this process in a live setting. For now, I need you to trust me as though I was teaching you to ride a bike. I want you to know that I am telling along with many others who have experienced this and will attest the same, that there is a universal power. Just start to take the steps even if you do not believe in it. Say the affirmations, find a support group or faithful community to be a part of. As you begin to practice and experience it, much as with riding a bike or swimming, it is almost inevitable you will experience it for yourself. Faith. This is a very important topic that is hardly ever discussed until you are involved in a marriage or serious relationship. But it is one of the most essential problems that most people deal with. I found it is one of my biggest limiters in life and as I overcome it, has become one of the most liberating skills you will learn. Now whether or not you really believe in God, religious communities on average strive for a healthier standard than our general population. Religious communities hold us accountable for our actions and create a support network for us which we can utilize in good times and in difficult times. It also promotes social interaction as we mentioned before. For kids it can additionally add to that microcosm that helps them create identity and find their place. It keeps us from most of the addictive and negative influences in our general society. So, I encourage you to explore this even if you do not believe in God, for the practical aspects of such a community, and because now we know this actually contributes to longevity and happiness. That's all I will say about it. My job is only to educate you. But then it is up to you entirely.

Prioritizing Family

We already talked a little bit about this but to emphasize again, one of the keys to a life of longevity and happiness is to prioritize family. This means being there in times of illness and happiness, sharing the burdens and victories that each person goes through. But, also as I said, it means giving importance to the job of raising a child. And that is what I want to reiterate. Most Blue Zoners put an emphasis on this. They understand that child rearing is one of the most important activities. I watched a comedian Ali Wong roast the women's liberation movement, but it holds some saddening truth. Home-stay women or men do not get proportionate retirement or disability benefits. Because of the increased costs of living, many women or families must be double income and still raise kids. But even with these rising living costs, I am glad to see the effort many families are making to be sure that children are the priority. This as I understood from research also promotes that children will grow up to care for elderly relatives which is crucial to happiness in old age. That continued involvement and respect in the final stage of life is what I believe vital in preventing depression amongst the elderly population. From witnessing the passing of many patients, I have learned that in the final moments, it is experiences and people that matter more than possessions or career success. In the final moments I have never heard a patient say I wish I had done better at work. Mostly it is I wish I had spent more time with a child or a spouse or other family. I am hoping we can understand this and as a society allow for that reprioritization of family again as most important versus career and money and find ways to actively engage the elderly in the upcoming years as our baby boomer population begins retiring.

Living in the Right Place

I find it interesting that the above-mentioned studies promote living in a healthy community that supports and promotes healthy physical lifestyle (11). I think this is a variable definition. It depends on what constitutes health and happiness for you. There are several areas in the U.S. now designated as Blue Zone Communities, so that is one option for healthy living. Consider that when I first came to California, I was most certainly ushered into a fitness gym almost immediately instead of the traditional neighborly welcome basket. But I also believe we must construe this principle as finding a locale that promotes a healthy lifestyle in general for you. For example, if you need to engage in a band as a hobby or career, then living in a metro environment that allows you to fulfill your core need to engage in that activity will be crucial. If traffic is highly stressful for you, then perhaps it wouldn't be a healthy environment. What I imagine with Blue Zone Research is that this category was meant specifically for physical health benefits listing areas that promote activity, but I feel it should go one step further to promote *both* health and happiness. Yes, living in a health-conscious society is important for longevity, but also living in a society that supports your goals in life is also important for your happiness. It would probably not be healthy if you lived in an income zone that did not match your own. You could get under great amounts of stress from trying to match a lifestyle above or below your earning level. Also living in an area that did not share your views say on cultural tolerance or on educational emphasis may cause stress unnecessarily. So, I think this is often something we can have great control over and many of us do not take advantage of this. Really sit down and think of what your own needs are and if the place where you live is meeting those needs as well as promoting health and activity.

Investing in Experiences

Our Western society is definitely more about possession versus experience. I am not sure why this is. Perhaps it is our way of anchoring ourselves. Or perhaps it is a more tangible way to prove our success. But in the studies, investment in experiences almost always reaped greater happiness than possessions (13). I wish this was of my own genius, but no, it is actually proven research. So, make the family trips, celebrate the birthdays, and live out your experiences. These are more meaningful than all the stuff, hard as it may be to believe.

Having a Purpose or Passion

Both groups of people who lived long and those who lived happy shared again this commonality of understanding their purpose and/or passion in life (14). Some people may say, I don't have a passion per se, but that is why I included here purpose or passion. These are two different things, but both can achieve a similar effect.

A purpose is another way to give meaning to the process of waking up and living out each day. If you always have that purpose in mind, then chances are less likely that depression will precipitate no matter what age you grow to be. Purpose is what I feel is the basic minimum. It is what I believe will decrease suicide rates.

Aside from knowing one's purpose, having a passion is an added way to give yourself meaning in life. Most people who engage with their passions find themselves from time to time in what is known as the "flow". While purpose involves what you yourself intend to do, passion involves your innate abilities and a higher connection with the universe. When you are engaging your passion, instead of being draining, it is actually; an energizing experience. Passion is what I feel is going above and beyond the minimum. This will keep you excited about living out each day. Improving your chances of living a long and healthy life are greatly increased by utilizing one or both these tools.

Giving & Receiving

People who live long and happy understand that giving is an important part of life. This can be done any number of ways, through donating time, money, or services. Try to find a way even if you have a busy schedule to give. One of the best pieces of advice I ever got was when you feel depressed about your life and can't find answers, don't try to solve your life, but try to solve someone else's. Help another person. This puts you in the line of the universal flow of giving and receiving and often as you help others you will that find solutions to your own problems may suddenly appear. This is the other secret that I find many successful and happy people know (15). They understand this cycle. Some refer to it as karma, others as the universal energy flow.

There is a misconception I have noticed in a lot of people who struggle with fate, destiny, and the higher powers that can be traced back to the principle of give and take. Many people believe this is a direct relationship. But from my experience, it is not. The popular book *The Secret*, gave celebrity status to the forces of the universe but I believe a lot of people do not grasp it fully. Most people see it two dimensionally, in that if I give I will get in return immediately and directly back from the universe. But in practice, most higher consciousness individuals will tell you that this is not the case, but rather is more like a spherical 3d globe of give and take. The give puts into motion effects which in some way or form will come back to you, but perhaps not in the way or form that you envision and perhaps not at the same time. This works in the other way too with bad energy. I want to add here that faith-based practices can take this to an even higher level. The best way I can relate it, is if you have a child on a swing they can propel themselves up and down, but by asking an adult to help, they can get a bigger push. Sometimes things they were not able to do on their own, with a faith-based approach, suddenly they may be able to achieve them. Since it is not a direct relationship and if you are asking how then to keep track and know if you are practicing this principle correctly, the best tip I have is to always try your best to do what you know is right, not necessarily what feels good. This will generally keep you on the "right" side of the universal flow.

The other part of this is that people who live long and happy also know how to receive from others and the universe. This is a highly overlooked issue. There are many people with guilt issues and insecurity that make them feel they are unworthy to receive or earn or be rewarded. This keeps them in a perpetual cycle of poverty and the feeling of unworthiness to live in comfort. It seems odd that someone would not want to live well, but our neurologic and psychiatric network is so interesting in that it tries to keep us in the familiar and not always the healthiest thought patterns. I recommend for people with these issues, to again utilize positive affirmations. Also, understand that when you have a strong foundation for yourself and are comfortable you are also able to give and help others more. Warren Buffett is an amazing example of this. He has identified his skill and passion and has been able to profit from it, but continues to live not according to his income, but according to what his needs are and gives the large majority of his fortune to help others. Abundance can be a good thing and if you understand the principle that you can help others by finding your own abundance, it helps to alleviate that engrained guilt that some of you have about receiving.

Genetics and Upbringing

So, let's blame our parents as usual for everything. We do actually have some genetic predilections for being happier and for having positive outlooks on life it would seem (21). But our environment and upbringing is also important and is key in influencing those outlooks as well. Warm loving childhoods definitely increase happiness levels according to research (22). And while this was not specifically stated in the Blue Zones Research for longevity, it was an implied factor. So, understand that your genetics are only the starting blocks but do not completely determine your level of happiness nor your outlook on life.

Diet

Ok, so most happiness studies as far I have seen, don't really get into a lot with diet which is why I left these sections for last. That being said; longevity studies showed this was a huge factor with all the groups. The main principle is that diet should be predominantly plant based. That means approximately 80% of the diet is plants and vegetables. I have read about and personally tried and studied so many different diets both as an individual and as a doctor. What I understand now is the no-carb diet is probably the most effective weight loss tool, but it is not a real sustainable way of life for anyone. I understand now that some good carbohydrates incorporated into the diet are necessary to temper the sugar cravings that we all get. By utilizing those good carbohydrates (brown rice, sweet potatoes, for example), our body decreases the desire for refined processed sugars. Our society has unknowingly or unconsciously created a system where it is difficult to avoid these sugar cravings. I won't say that I am perfect either, it's tough avoiding sodas and desserts. I am definitely not there yet myself, but I have greatly advanced in the process. But it is as they say is a lifestyle choice. As you begin to make some changes, it will get easier and easier and you will enjoy it more and more. Then you will actively seek out those elements and you will begin to find that it simplifies your life choices, because at least in this time and society, those healthier options are usually very limited.

We are now seeing new research that links cancer with high protein diets and with high dairy intake. The Blue Zone model recommends minimizing protein to very small amounts (approximately less than 5 times per month) (1). I won't tell you there is a definitive link between protein intake and cancer because while you may see one research study that will argue for this hypothesis, you will see another research study that will argue the opposite hypothesis. What I can tell you is that none of the blue zone groups ate any large quantities of protein (1, 16, 17) and only one group ate significant amounts of dairy (Sardinians love cheese and milk products). I can only recommend following what the masters of longevity are doing which is to keep with high amounts of plants and vegetables and very limited amounts of protein and refined sugars. As for the milk and dairy products, it seems that it may increase certain types of cancers while decreasing the risk for other types of cancers, perhaps this could play into why Sardinian men live so long. However, as for my own recommendation, I think because evidence points to arguments that dairy can increase some cancers and decrease others, perhaps a moderate intake (no more than 2 glasses of milk per day) until we have more definitive evidence is my own professional recommendation (17). And if you are already someone with high risk for a certain type of cancer genetically or based on family predisposition, maybe check if dairy could increase your risks in those specific circumstances. I think we need more research on why the Sardinians in particular, are able to outlive others with such a diet. We may not be able to understand the science behind these diets for some time because we need much more controlled studies to discern how many confounding factors exist such as how hormone additions, pesticides, and refined food processing and storage are affecting our diet. But these Blue Zone societies are still outliving the rest of us in a modern time. So, I think it is safe to at least model their plans especially using the plant-based approach until we do understand the science. I know it is hard, I love meals with meat too, but as you start to practice it you will feel you have an amazing secret that others just aren't privy to. You will feel good when you put it in practice.

Another note on diet which I felt was very strongly common amongst all the groups was the intake of tea. Specifically, green or white tea. These groups drink tea throughout the day at least 4-5 cups. Black tea seems to contain too much caffeine, so it must be green or white tea, another reason I like calling it "Getting into the Green Zone". The reason behind this commonality I speculate is that tea encourages water intake but uses small amounts of caffeine which may help with boosting metabolism and weight loss. I do have to caution that studies have shown drinking large amounts of overly hot liquids can be linked to throat and esophageal cancers. So as a warning to those of you about to start downing the tea, please be cautious to make sure your tea is not too hot. Specific temperatures where the risk for cancers are noted to increase are above 65 degrees Celsius or 149 degrees Fahrenheit (19). You can invest in a tea thermometer, but as you will probably not carry it around with you, the rule of thumb is to wait at least 4 minutes before drinking your freshly brewed tea.

Alcohol, I want to touch on as well, and I really debated putting this in here. But as I pledged to share the secrets of longevity and happiness, I must report the findings as such. As a doctor, I tend not to promote alcohol to my patients. This is because of the devastating effects of chronic alcoholism including liver failure and pancreatitis and so many cancer associations. Additionally, I have observed that most patients already intake a moderate amount of alcohol. But in keeping with the topic of this book, the millennials as per Buettner's research, do drink moderate amounts of alcohol socially, except those in Loma Linda who strictly avoid it. I want to emphasize that it is only a moderate amount of alcohol that seems to help with heart health and that is recommended by this longevity study (1). In fact, the American Heart Association currently still does not recommend people to start drinking alcohol due to high risk for alcoholism, even with research that alcohol may decrease the risk of heart events, (20). If you are already an alcoholic and have an unhealthy relationship with alcohol, this guideline is probably not the one you want to pick up on. Remember moderation is the key to the essence of longevity. Moderation means an average of one to two drinks per day for men and one drink per day for women. (A drink is one 12 oz. beer, 4 oz. of wine, 1.5 oz. of 80-proof spirits, or 1 oz. of 100-proof spirits.) (20).

Exercise

Again, this is primarily more emphasized in the research on longevity than in happiness studies. However, plenty of research exists that relates exercise with positive endorphins which theoretically should lead to better levels of happiness (11). Exercise in the setting of the blue zone research was only recommended at a moderate daily level, usually incorporated into our daily activities (1). Now there are some cities in our own country that are newly designated Blue Zone societies after Dan Buettner's research that uses blue zone principles by incorporating these principles at a governmental and infrastructural level (18). This means that people may be encouraged to walk between work and home or school and home. I think this is great and in a short time frame, these measures are already demonstrating a lot of great results. But not all of us are fortunate enough to live in these areas where these principles are seamlessly incorporated in our day to day life. So, yes moderate daily activity is recommended, but what if it isn't a part of your daily activity? Some of us will need to still create work-out regimens that will get us that needed activity. The research does not seem to encourage intense fitness regimens, but you have to examine your overall activity levels and decide if you are really engaging in 30 mins to an hour of physical activity a day. If you do not, perhaps, working out 3-4 days a week in a gym is going to be important for you.

Gardening

I put here a special note on Gardening, because I know this is a practice that few Americans really engage in, but one that almost all Blue Zone Millennials do engage in. I don't have a green thumb, but I intend to put this into practice as well. My theory is that gardening increases oxygenation and promotes relaxation. It also creates a sense of purpose, patience, and self-reward. I want to promote this practice. So, whether you grow a single flower or a whole garden, try it out and see if the benefits are there for you.

This ends my discussion of the basic principles of "Getting into The Green Zone". From here I will go into an advanced discussion of Green Zone Living and how to achieve it.

Before we move on, let's recap the main principles of both Longevity and Happiness and the most critical overlaps that will get us into the Green Zone. All the factors in the diagram will help you to achieve a long life and a happy life, but the central concepts seem to be especially crucial in both areas.

Getting Into The Green Zone

Live Long

- Avoid Overeating (80% rule)
- Primarily Plant based diet
- Moderate daily exercise
- Moderate alcohol intake
- Live in a society that promotes health and activity
- Engage in a faith based community ritual
- Marriage and family are considered priority
- Gardening
- Drink Tea often

Supportive Social Relationships

Positive Outlook on Life

Finding Passion in and for life

Stress Reducing Activities

Live Happy

- Genetic predisposition
- Loving Childhood
- Learn how to both give and receive from life and others.
- Be proactive and Do not procrastinate
- Do not be limited by your fears
- Invest in experiences over owning things
- Practicing Gratefulness

Advanced Green Zone Principles

Optimizing health

The factors I discussed previously were general principles which apply to anyone and everyone. Now we will talk about how to approach individual issues that potentially will keep you from achieving lifelong health and happiness.

I spent a lot of time talking about my two types of patients for a reason. I want to show that most of us are stuck in one of two unhealthy paths. We should focus not on maintaining health or preventing injury and illness but as with a child learning to solve problems, expecting illness and injury and how to address and move forward from that. Everyone gets sick and gets injured. Imagine if someone told you that you had a 100% chance of getting rained on today, then you would probably prepare by wearing the right clothes or bringing an umbrella with you. And it is unlikely that you would be very upset by rain. However, take the same situation, especially in California, where you just were not expecting the rain. If it rained on you suddenly, you would probably be upset or have a reaction that would be likely annoyance, frustration, or anger. You might not have worn the right type of shoes or gotten your hair done and now it has all gotten ruined. See how expectation and preparation can drastically alter your experience of the same event.

I realize now that people do not treat the medical field this way. They expect to be healthy always, which is unrealistic, or to always be sick, which is also not accurate. We need to familiarize ourselves to the cycles of life. Just as the economy goes up and down, our health will do the same. In times of health, we need to enjoy it and understand this is not an eternal state of life. We also need to prepare in those times by addressing our minor health issues and life situation so that when illness does hit, we know we have done our best in creating a foundation where we do not crumble. What does this mean practically? Practically, this means getting checked not only when we feel bad, but also yearly checking in with our doctor and working on our health proactively. This means searching in our family history or our own background for conditions we might be at risk for and taking steps to decrease our chances of having complications related to those things. We also need to determine what things will optimize our health and physical fitness. Lastly, we need to strengthen our spiritual, economic, and social circles so that our medical illness will not be our downfall.

Let me give you an example from my own experience. I talked about my terrible allergies. I went through every line of allergy medications known, each worked temporarily. Finally, I ended up on shots. Allergy shots are wonderful, they are just highly expensive and extremely inconvenient. I suppose being a physician I might have given them to myself, but I didn't want to go into an extreme allergic reaction and end up having to treat myself. It probably would not have happened, but if I haven't mentioned it before, one of my ultimate goals is to not die of stupidity. Instead I had the experience that all my patients had, which was to go to an Allergy specialist. During this time, I got hit with big bills as copays for each of my shots which was 2x a week for a year. Additionally, I got scars on my arms from an overaggressive dosing schedule and difficulties with insurance and office policies quickly got me fed up with the shots I needed. Yes, I needed those shots, without them, I was a mess stashing perpetually a pack of tissue on me, and every time I entered a new environment I spent about 10 minutes sneezing my way into acclimatization. After I got fed up with the allergy shot scheme, I investigated other new options for treatment of allergies. And I stumbled upon what was an old form of treatment, not quite as effective but deemed fairly effective. These were allergy drops that you could do at home. So, I tried the process and followed the apparent dosing schedule and now I no longer carry tissue with me at all, and I hardly ever sneeze or have the old symptoms I used to be plagued by unless I change cities entirely, which is when I must re-titrate my regimen. What's even more was that this treatment did not treat just the symptoms of my affliction, it treated the core issue of what was causing my issue without sedation and was significantly cheaper than the shots I was getting, I was able to get them no matter my travel or work schedule, and I could do it from home safely.

Why hadn't I learned of this years ago? Why? It's because I had to get to a point of desperation to consider other treatments, to find out other options and alternatives. I want to encourage people not to get to that point of desperation. I want people to use their periods of health to evaluate problems they have and make sure these problems are optimized. Look for ways to improve what is considered an ok, but less than ideal situation. Now, I don't want people to have false hopes, because there are conditions that we just don't have treatments for, but I do know that almost every problem that exists in the world has been experienced by someone else. If there is not a solution or cure for the problem itself already, there may be in the least a likely way to improve your level of life or to improve your symptoms.

So here I encourage you to write down the current medical problems you have and see what is optimal in your life and what is not. If it is not, really do some research to find out if there is anything you can do to optimize your health. Secondly, write down your biggest fears when it comes to illness and major disability. Once you have those fears, talk to your friends, a spouse, a counselor, or research some ways to address those fears and lack of preparation. Then take steps to strengthen yourself for those situations. The reason why this book would only work right now is that it is only recently that we have at our fingertips access to these vast stores of information, not only from published works but from every person who has experienced or dealt with an affliction. All of this is available to us. I encourage you to do research, ask questions, and seek out answers. This is also how I found the right products to treat my skin disorder even when that was well before the time of the internet and took a lot more effort. But I ventured out and found people who had my same condition and found out what they were doing. Now Crisco thankfully is only for cooking. In using the same approach, you may find ways to address some or many of your problems.

Now what about in times of illness? If you have prepared for illness as you should in your times of health, you will not have as many feelings of anger and frustration about illness as if you had gotten caught in the rain. Understanding that illness is an expected part of life is very important. My own dental issues I learned later in life was a product of recurrent tonsillitis and bronchitis that resulted in mouth breathing for many years but my fault or not, those are complications that I will have to face my entire life. I now must prepare for this reality, but that preparation is helpful because it doesn't surprise or shock me any longer. And believe me almost everyone must learn to deal with their own individual issues. Some of us learn to deal with this early on and others later in life, but when you can recognize that everyone must deal with their own set of issues, you will feel much more comfort that you are not being punished or that your situation is singularly horrible.

But now let's say you are reading this book and you are already in a state of poor health or dealing with an immediate medical issue. What do you do now? I recommend to still write down your medical problems in their entirety. Our goal is to first address the most immediate problems and ones that are causing you the most stress. But by writing down all the problems, you have quickly and efficiently in an instant taken the pressure from your mind about having to solve all of them. The mind is very interesting, and it loves solving problems. So, once you designate something as a problem, your mind consciously and unconsciously goes to work trying to solve those problems. But if you actively and physically make a step to tell your mind it does not have to worry about a problem because it will be addressed, even if at a later time, your mind can let go quite a bit. The simple act of writing a problem down on a list signals this to your mind. That is why so many top executives and professionals still use hand written notes to keep organized. And the reason we are doing this is because we need to harness the focus and energy of our mind and body into solving one or two main problems while at the same time employing an immediate stress reducing technique.

Many of us struggle also with procrastination. Happier people tend not to procrastinate. The reason we tend to procrastinate often is because of having so many tasks to accomplish. I'm no exception, especially in this age of technology which has a plethora of information and no downtime in which to process all of it. This creates overwhelm which then causes us to not complete any tasks. So instead, focus on one thing. This is the other extremely important skill (aside from learning faith and trust), that will help you immeasurably in achieving all sorts of goals. But I am utilizing this focus to try to address medical issues. By allowing yourself to focus on the one or two immediate problems you have, you will allow yourself and your doctor the opportunity to find the best options for your most immediate issue.

I have found oftentimes because of the new healthcare system that has put more and more requirements and legal responsibilities onto physicians, it allows them less freedom and time to talk with and research the problems of their patients. There are unrealistic expectations about what a physician can actually do in the time they are able to work with patients. Let's say, you hired a trainer. Nobody expects their bodies will be perfect after working out with them for one session. In fact, typically people meet with a trainer at least 3 times per week for an hour. But somehow with a doctor, patients often expect them to solve all their lifelong problems in 15 minutes.

So use your annual physical exams to discuss those less pressing issues and focus on the immediate problems during follow up visits. But do not let this stop you researching on your own possibilities to address issues in the interim. Before, information was not readily available, so you had to wait to speak to doctors and specialists in order to find out what new advances and treatment options were available. On the other hand, also understand that just because you find a treatment doesn't mean it is appropriate for you. I still suggest you discuss with your medical professional any major treatments you want to try. If it is a new procedure or treatment, your doctor may also need time to look into the effectiveness and the complications of it and if it is applicable in your particular situations. To let you know how many things need to be considered, for any treatment as simple as a cream or pill, and MD will have to consider liver function, kidney function, hormonal changes, side effects of the medication and potential interactions the medication may have with the other medicines you are on at a minimum. So even when a treatment may seem promising, it may be that it's not suitable for you specifically because of one of these factors.

Optimizing Social Relationships

Considering how important social relationships are to both longevity and happiness as the research studies would make it appear, I really want to spend some time on this topic. When people say they are loners, it usually means there exists an underlying fear of social rejection. If you are a person that has difficulty having or keeping close relationships, you should consider talking with a professional about why this is the case. Relationships as you have seen make up the majority of what creates a healthy and happy life. It is incredible that most of us have deep seated issues with this. I myself was a very quiet person when I was young and I learned to be more outspoken, but I have always been social. I took for granted that everyone knew how to be or even wanted to be social. Now I realize that there are many people that truly struggle with this. Other signs of this are people highly sensitive to comments and criticism who react with anger, contempt, or violence. But even as I am social, I also have strong issues with confidence that led me to find circumstances that reconfirmed my own low self-esteem for many years. It was only until years later that I fully understood this cycle and finally having discovered my own problems that I could get out of this cycle and take steps to address those problems. I now strongly recommend mental health as maintenance for everyone. The same way we expect our bodies to run into problems through the years, we can expect to have mental health issues of anxiety, stress, depression, or unhealthy behaviors we have developed even from childhood and others we acquired in adolescence and adulthood. I encourage us as a society to remove the stigma of mental health being a negative thing. Mental health should be at least as important as physical health and yet we avoid dealing with mental health like a plague. Medicine is currently in a maintenance phase where people are starting to address problems routinely by doing preventative screening. Before this phase our parents practiced survival medicine, where we only went to the doctor when we were sick and couldn't function. Well mental health practices are still a step behind and currently we practice survival mental health where we only seek out help when those issues are so strong that we can no longer function. In reality, there are few people who can probably walk around saying that they are emotionally healthy and stable. It is my opinion that you are more likely to have mental health issues even over physical health issues. Why is that? It is because our minds and our neural pathways are in large part formed by the people and experiences we have as a very small child. Our physical health, however, is generally independent of the influence of others and is essentially a mold made from our genetic hardware. What happens to that mold is almost entirely dependent on our own choices. It is akin to something like a new smartphone which is only affected by our own individual actions, differing from our mental health software which is constantly absorbing reprogramming based on stimulation from our surroundings. This means even when we start out with healthy minds and souls we absorb the angst, mindsets, and responses of the people we are surrounded with. Ultimately, we must face that we are highly prone to unhealthy behaviors and responses and insecurities. Even when consciously you may feel one way, subconsciously your mind and body are programmed differently. This creates the core conflict between values and belief. One of those is our true and pure inclinations, but the other was instilled in us from our environment. And often those two concepts do not match which creates in many of us constant struggles that muddies our decisions and creates anxiety in us over the disparity between the two. Social relationships can often highlight these disparities and the insecurity over them.

You have heard over and over that we are designed to be social. In fact, even though technology is a new tool, it is still the core concept of networking and connections that run the world. Solitary is one of the worst punishments we can imagine as humans because we require social interaction. This is why "loners" are usually avoiding dealing with deep seated insecurities typically about rejection and acceptance and tend to stay away from situations that risk either one of them. I'm not saying that being alone isn't good sometimes but avoidance of social relationships is unhealthy.

If this describes you or you find certain types of relationships are causing a lot of stress and anxiety, there are some tips I can give to help you become a more social person. The first tip is to never assume anything about anyone. You never know what has happened to a person even 5 minutes before you meet them. Perhaps they found out their mother had died. Or perhaps they were served with divorce papers. Perhaps they failed a test. I think I gained this from reading a lot of science fiction and fantasy novels. Every person has a logic, has a story. You may not understand where they are coming from and why they react the way they do. But it is assured that they operate on a logic that if you were privy to all the details of their story you would completely understand why they make the very decisions that they do. In fact if you learned their story you may even find that you often would probably do the exact same things if you were in the same position. Understanding this principle makes meeting people an exciting adventure. If you don't try to like or accept someone or have anticipation that they must like or accept you, and instead just try to learn their story, you will find the emotional pressure of relationships is suddenly removed. Each person is like a storybook. I personally find this interesting and fascinating. And just like a story, there is always a who, what, when, where, why and how. You can use these same concepts to find ways to talk to people. When you don't know what to say, think of these questions and try to come up with questions that will help you learn about these core components of a person's life. For example, imagine if a person reveals they have two children. A great bridge to conversation is to delve further into that topic. People typically reveal on the surface the most important and least threatening things about themselves. So you can probably figure that this person feels proud of being a parent or at least comfortable with their identity as a parent. Great follow up questions would be to ask how old the kids are, what their names are, and if they are planning to have more, what hobbies they enjoy, or how their experience of being a parent is. You can even then ask about what type of family they themselves grew up in and if they have multiple brothers or sisters. This may seem like a basic and intuitive thing to do, but when you understand the principle of why this works without just taking it for granted, it will help you in times where things are not so straightforward. Always try to find the story.

Having said this, I can attest to the fact that when you find a person who is truly interested in your story, that person really stands out. Asking questions isn't the only skill to learn. Listening is a much harder skill to attain, especially in the U.S. culture where we tend to be impatient and where we are uncomfortable with silence. In this country every second has to be filled with words or actions. But learning to let someone talk until they finish, will help you stand out as a person who truly cares and who is truly listening. That is a rare quality in our society and I admit I struggle with this often trying to fill in people's sentences or suggest answers for them when they stop to think of what they are trying to say.

Once you acquire these two skills of engaging in conversation and listening, another tool to increasing patience around different types of personalities is to also understand that inside everyone is a child. We may have adult bodies, but we are all still looking for those basic child needs of acceptance, love, security, and praise. So, when people react harshly or in ways you find distasteful, if you stop for a second, you can probably identify that those behaviors are usually coming from a place of insecurity where one of those core needs have been threatened. By using this approach, you can find compassion for that person instead of hatred and disgust. It is easier to see a child throw a tantrum versus an adult but it is the same principle. I am not saying allow yourself to be abused or walked over, but in the mean time you can retain your self-respect and dignity, you can have some patience for others who do not have that for themselves.

Lastly another tip to helping you become social is understanding again the principle of a table. Stress is a tangible but invisible health factor. If you look at handling a ton of stress on your own, you can imagine how stress can create in us insomnia, and neck and back problems and headaches and all sorts of other physical ailments. But I propose that the reason that social people can stay alive longer and be happier is because they understand that like ants carrying a large object, sharing the burden of problems makes it a lighter burden to handle. This doesn't mean you need to tell all your dirty laundry to the world; but confiding some of your concerns to close friends or just receiving listening and confirmation of your feelings can help remove the heavy burden. Even finding another person who has the same problem can give you additional strength to deal with the problem and to confirm you are not crazy and you are having normal reactions and feelings which in turns gives the ability to deal better with your problems.

I realized from my own experiences it's not having many friends or even just one good friend that is the key to this social necessity. It is our need to have a place and to feel important. You could have a hundred friends but if they are not essential to affirming that you are the person you identify yourself as, their presence is not crucial. Why also is it not enough to only have a good loving spouse for example? It is not enough because our place in the world usually cannot be defined by only one person. That person would have to affirm all corners of your personality to be the only person involved in this definition. Definition of oneself is very complex and typically requires multiple facets of identity to be confirmed. Usually this requires groups of people and a stable environment to produce. So, creating a community doesn't only mean finding a place to live and making friends in order to produce happiness or longevity. It means you must identify with a group that affirms your place in the world in a positive manner. The Okinawans actually have lifelong groups typically of 4-5 friends who serve especially in this type of role.

Optimizing Stress Reduction

That brings us to more advanced principles of stress reduction. Yoga and meditation are two of the best stress reducing practices. I think there are other things you can do to really improve in this area. The first one is a totally personal exercise investigating your personal triggers. We tend to speak of triggers in terms of relationships. And I delved into this a bit before. But I want to utilize this as a general principle. If you can understand the things that cause you stress at the onset, then you can avoid and decrease the actual incidence of those things in your life. When you have allergies for example, the best thing you can do is to avoid the offending agent. Similarly, the best form of stress reduction is to prevent it. You can do this by identifying what are known as triggers. These are the events and circumstances that put you personally into a state of high anxiety and frustration. For example, as I mentioned before I do not like being late, so I purposefully forward my clocks so that I am generally able to be on time. I also do not like being rushed into doing activities so I always allot myself ample time to complete each task. My spouse has a whole other set of triggers, but in addressing his triggers as my own, we both benefit from lower stress levels.

Along the same lines, outside of your primary relationship, you can apply the same principle to every day interactions.

Instead of just saying that someone else caused you to be angry or upset or nervous, a proactive approach of identifying moments where you are distressed can help you to create a new way to deal with those emotions. Much of the time the actions we relate to as annoying to the point we get emotional is usually built up resentment about actions or experiences from the past. Learning about those specific things can help to lessen the frustration when encountering those situations and improve your chances of responding in an emotionally healthy manner further lessening stress created by the situation and by lessening the rebounding guilt that we feel when we know we responded in a way that is not in keeping with our best.

Understanding those triggers also helps us plan for those situations by allowing us to create options for a different response. Let's think of it like emergency preparedness. When a natural disaster happens, we typically have some idea of what we should do. In a fire, we exit the building in an orderly manner, stay close to the ground, and avoid touching metal objects. These steps may seem obvious but in fact for most of us they have been taught to us in schools and then engrained in us. It was only then that those behaviors became "obvious". So, when an actual fire occurs, though we still will have levels of panic and stress coursing through our veins, we will respond with those entrained actions and produce a better result. Each trigger can be treated like a different natural disaster. You don't respond the same way for a fire as for a tornado or hurricane. Similarly, each trigger must be addressed independently and "escape" mechanisms created for each one. This may seem tedious and time consuming, but the other big part of creating a peaceful and happy life is planning. Business owners realize this after their failures. Planning is the key to execution and finesse in any venture. People believe taking a week to look at triggers and thinking of ways to reduce stress and increase efficiency may be ridiculous. But think of how much time you have in the past spent planning a wedding, a vacation, or even a birthday party in your life. I can almost assure that you spent probably a week or two planning those small parts of your life. To spend a week or two thinking of how to restructure and implement your everyday life is not asking a lot and is worth the time investment.

Additionally, the people I know that do this actually look forward to it. They view it as a time of reflection, relaxation, and energizing. Often, they plan to do it in accordance with a trip that gives them alone time or couple time that helps them to think and plan. In those settings such as spending a day on the beach just thinking of your life and how you can improve the inefficiencies and decrease the stress by specific actions, it can turn into a truly enjoyable tradition. And yes, this probably needs to be done not just once, but time to time. The most successful people I know do this every 6 months to a year. High level CEOs do this in the business world almost once a week but using a smaller scale of planning times from one hour to a half day.

Having talked about couples' trips, I also think it is important for you to consider doing this strategy session with anyone who is largely affected by your decisions and who will largely impact you with their decisions. This is often a spouse or partner but could possibly be parents or children. Why do I suggest this? It is important to understand that while you may have a logical plan to address things in your own life, others can hinder or advance your projects and goals. In addition, talking about your triggers and stressors with the very people who often are involved can help you explain to them those situations in a way that they can have compassion for you and so that you both can come up with a plan to avoid those situations or address them in a different way. Doing this at a specific time where you are discussing any and all issues instead of in the heated moment brings more understanding and creative solutions and reduces the emotional component that is usually attached at the time of the argument or disagreement. Of course, not all issues will be able to wait for such a time, but many can wait. Make sure to write them in a book or journal so you don't lose track of those issues that need to be addressed.

Journaling is another advanced way of stress reduction. This may be hard for some who do not like to write. But I bring this up because writing allows an emotional release as well as stimulates an internal discussion that can lead to epiphanies and solutions to various problems.

If you haven't done this, then just start by writing freehand all your feelings down, good, bad and ugly. You may get emotional doing this, but then go back and read what you have written as an outsider. This will allow you the perspective of compassion for yourself. I also encourage you to truly learn to have compassion for yourself. Many of us are hard on ourselves and on others because we don't understand that it is okay to be compassionate. When someone lends you compassion, even if it comes from yourself, the anger, hurt and resentment of a situation can greatly lessen. As I discussed before, sharing stress with others can lessen that burden, and that includes yourself even if you are the only person you can share it with.

Now letting go of resentment is another topic to discuss with regards to stress reduction. Resentment is a main cause of unnecessary stress. It took a lot of understanding on my part to understand how to release and let go of resentment. While journaling can lessen stress and identifying triggers can prevent stress, addressing resentment is getting to the core causative agents that create stress. How do you let go of resentment? Letting go of resentment requires you to understand the core part of yourself from which the resentment stems from. Do you blame someone or yourself for something? Ask yourself, what core idea or representation that you identify yourself with was challenged by that action or comment? After answering this, then ask, how can you rectify or change this idea you have and where a single comment, situation, or action confirmed your fears. Let's take for example, many years ago when my husband wanted to eat only vegetarian foods. Of course, at that time, I had no concept of eating a meal with no meat. The concept of having to create healthy fresh meals was already challenging enough for me. Still with much difficulty, I finally figured it out by the time I had a baby. But when my husband no longer wanted meat as a part of our diet, this new request to change diet was overwhelming for me. It was my husband's core idea of not eating foods that promoted inhumane treatment of animals that challenged my own difficult core idea that a mother should be able to prepare healthy fresh meals for the whole family, so I became resentful of my husband. I shouldn't have been resentful, because he was trying to think of the health of our family and not asking anything unreasonable. There are plenty of vegetarians in the world; but I didn't know how to reconcile those two concepts, and shortly thereafter I became resentful. What it took me some time to understand was that I wasn't resentful of the fact that I couldn't eat meat, I was truly resentful that I didn't know how to cook balanced healthy vegetarian meals and that in my own mind this meant I didn't know how to be the mother I felt I needed or wanted to be. It had nothing to do with the meat! So, while you could say fear comes from lack of preparedness, resentment comes from a challenge to a core belief by an opposing idea, belief, comment, or situation. Again, they both stem from insecurity or instability in our beliefs about ourselves. If I had no doubt about my maternal nature or being a good mother, my husband's request to change our family diet would have just caused me to ask myself how to achieve the goal without the resentment that went along with it. So, for all the issues that bring up resentment, try again to identify what part of your core belief, value, or identity has been violated or challenged or even abandoned. Then you must really work on correcting that disparity. You can correct this disparity by either affirmations that dispute those insecurities in your head. Or you can take concrete actions that will bridge the gap that creates those insecurities. Also remember that often the resentment is not actually with the other person, often it is really that we resent ourselves.

Lastly, let's talk about sleep and rest. You might say this is a basic stress reduction technique, but I consider it advanced. What many of us do not understand is that sleep is the vehicle by which our creative mind takes over. We cement memories, reenergize our brains, and allow our creative patterns to work. See, even unconsciously, our brain is wired to solve problems. Often our unconscious can work to solve problems even as our conscious brain cannot find solutions. I think of it like when my computer updates overnight. Suddenly small problems that existed before have been worked out or new useful features pop up where they were nonexistent the day before. Fatigue can often prevent us from finding those answers or from allowing the creative centers of our brain to take over. So, when a problem seems unsolvable, often just taking a nap or putting the problem to bed for a day, you can find answers to stressful questions and problems. And of course, resolving the underlying fatigue will also reduce stress directly.

This may sound funny coming from a doctor that worked nights for many years. But while I was able to get ample rest before having a child in the daytime, with a family schedule this became an increasing problem that affected my weight as chronic fatigue set in. Children don't like the nocturnal schedule. I want you to consider if you are able to get adequate sleep whenever that may be.

Advanced Principles of Exercise

Moderate exercise is important, but, remember that the body is like any machine. While it has this magical ability to recuperate, that doesn't mean it is invincible. Seems simple, but I didn't even understand this until not too long ago. I didn't think of the effects of my specific actions; just that in exercising and eating right as all doctors advise, that our bodies would be fine. But think of your body more like an expensive machine, more like a car. Don't abuse it. Remember that repetitive actions cause wear and tear, just like if you continually rub a corner of a suitcase. Don't abuse any one part of your body, try to learn proper techniques over quantity of exercises in the beginning. This will give you better results and keep you from injury and wear and tear. Consider changing your exercise regimens day to day to avoid over-stressing any one particular joint or part of the body.

Lastly, with regards to exercise, I want to emphasize here an understanding of different types of exercise. There is cardio training which focuses on the heart and circulatory system and requires a high caloric burning for a short period of time. There is also resistance or weight training which focuses on lower caloric burning but builds muscle over time. Those muscles then keep a continual low level caloric burn throughout the day. There are other less emphasized training elements which should be mentioned, balance training is important especially as we age to help us prevent falls and injuries. Tai chi is very focused on this important part of exercise. Lastly flexibility training helps prevent injuries and can act to counter the normal effects of daily activity on the spine and musculoskeletal structures. Yoga and certain yoga poses are designed to increase flexibility but can also lengthen the spine. You can even regain up to 1 to 2 inches of lost spinal height from doing these types of activities.

I mention all these different types of exercise here because I want to introduce you to an age old but an important theme I am revisiting throughout this book and employing in all my consulting practices. I believe one of our biggest mistakes is that in almost every field we tend to focus on one area. We do this because it is easy, convenient, or because we don't understand how important all of them are. This was not a concept I gained from any one of these research lines but from general life study and various lines of research and noticing a common unstated theme. We must engage all the legs of balance in order to create a stable foundation. In exercise this is no different. Please try to incorporate all these forms of training at various times into your workouts or daily activities to maintain and optimize your physical fitness.

I wonder at times if we shouldn't also focus on another type of training. I watch my young son in Tae Kwon Do class and they spend a lot of time on learning to fall. It was just fun to watch at first, but another reason I am writing this book is because I hope to provoke thought and inspire others and perhaps doing fall training in the elderly or at even earlier ages would be an important type of focused training that will help us achieve longevity and happiness to a greater degree. I often find that my patients that are above 90 are decrepit and have poor quality of life. My observation is that this is greatly related to mobility issues, so I think this effort to avoid injury and disability could really help our aging society.

Optimizing Finances

This is a difficult topic for many people. People think having money will solve problems. But as wise gurus will tell you, you will never make more money until you learn to manage the money you have right now. Happiness is only affected by money in so much as their basic needs must be met. As I want to emphasize with many of the topics in this book, balance is again key. Put into play the principles of saving, investing, spending, budgeting, and paying off debt. It is similar to the balance of a fitness regimen between cardio and aerobic exercise. If you do one or the other, you can have a fair level of health but cannot reach the optimal level without utilizing all these principles.

Here I will not tell you to try to make a million dollars. I am not here in the respect of being the type of consultant who will advise you on how to just get what you want. It's easy to realize that most of us want the same things in a dream world. We want to be rich and famous and beautiful while living in the most modern biggest homes with someone doing all the things we don't want for us and traveling first class all the time. But the reality is a different story. Let me tell you a story of how I became a celebrity for a short time. My uncle lives in the South of India and there he is known as Captain Raju. He acted in and produced Malayalam and Tamil movies primarily. Although he is not a Bollywood actor, he is a fairly prominent celebrity in South India. This was evident every time he would greet us in India. At the airport, suddenly my family was surrounded by a large ring of people. And subsequently anytime my Uncle was around, people would be following and watching us. Now, thankfully people aren't as aggressive in a fanatic sense in South India as they are in the U.S., but the feeling of no privacy is not really something I care for. The feeling of always having to represent perfection is not something I would like the pressure of, even though there are some perks to being famous like getting the best seating at restaurants and other perks that are rather nice. So, I am here as a doctor helping you to get what you want but more importantly than that, directing you to identify first what you need. I think a big fallacy with many coaches is trying to coach you into success without understanding what the definition of success really is for each person. It is not the same thing for each person. I like to use lots of analogies, so if I was a life coach telling you that Christian Louboutin shoes were the pinnacle of success, I could be right. However, if you needed to go out and play a championship basketball game, then guiding you to that conclusion would probably be the wrong thing. The most important part of getting into the green zone is the part that most people and coaches forget or are unaware of. That concept is an in-depth and insightful understanding of oneself.

In terms of finances, you must understand what your needs are first. As much as happiness may not vary in the meantime basic needs are met, perhaps we must admit that basic needs may be different for each person. Some people may feel owning a home is a basic necessity. But Matthew McConaughey for many years did not have that necessity despite having enough money to buy any sort of home he wanted. It was only when he had a family he felt the need to have a home. Before that he lived reportedly in a trailer so that he could surf on the beach. That is why it is not necessarily important that you make more than what you make now. It is not important that you make a million dollars either. What is important is that you make what you need in order to meet all the important aspects of your life comfortably. To do this you must first define all the important components of your life. Then you must understand the costs of maintaining all those important components. You must also understand that life is a fluid thing and these necessities can change. However, if you can anticipate some certain changes that most people go through, you can avoid realizing later that your income which used to be sufficient no longer is sufficient. Again, I compare this to a vacation. You research and investigate the costs depending on where you are going, how much hotels and taxis cost and what level of luxury you can accept and afford and what do certain activities cost. Based on this you make decisions on where you stay, how much you spend shopping or on excursions. But in life, we don't do this kind of planning which is why many people find themselves unable to mesh their practical reality with their ideal lifestyle and then face the stress and subsequent health consequences that grow from that disparity. I really think this sort of planning should be done when we are young adults as soon as we have the mental maturity to think about our future so it can help us decide our career paths and school choices and other major decisions in life.

Another important principle for successful financial health is to focus on achieving financial freedom. This gives you knowledge that no matter the economy, you will not have to worry about debt to another person which keeps you from taking risks and potentially achieving your full potential. Set a plan on how you will become financially free. Credit is a tool but should not be a set of chains. Buy only what you can afford and use credit only when you know you can pay it back.

Motivation & Effecting Change

These things are easier to plan as a young person before setting out on a certain path, which is why I want to work with enlightened parents and motivated youngsters to create those paths from the beginning. But it is never too late to learn. People get a misconception that it is harder to learn as an adult. I think this is partly true. I think it is less natural to learn as an adult than as a child. Our whole youth is about learning. Even playing is a form of learning. As an adult, supposedly we should have learned already and know what to do. But I hold a slightly different opinion in that I realize all my medical school training occurred after the age of 21. I had no knowledge of it before then. Additionally, most of the people in my class were much older than me and in fact many of them turned out to be better learners than myself because they had more understanding into why they were learning. We also have a saying in medical school which is "See One, Do One, and Then Teach One". It can be scary to learn something new but it can be done. The first step is to know that something can be done and watch it being done. Then you must master the skills required to do the task on your own, and then finally teach another person how to do the same task. It is when you teach, you really become an expert because you must know all the person's doubts and questions and the answers to those questions which means you must know all the ins and outs of the situation. All of this is to say that it doesn't matter at what age you start to learn a new language, you must realize first that you can learn and change at any time. It may not feel comfortable or easy, but you can do it. Then you need to find the resources or people to teach you those new skills, and then you must put it into practice and hopefully become a master yourself so you can teach someone else too.

The other part of effecting change is having the motivation to change. In medical practice, it is recommended not to push patients to quit smoking until they themselves show motivation to quit. There is a reason for this. Someone who is not motivated for any reason will not have a high rate of success in attempting any new ventures. So, I encourage you not to just jump into a weight loss plan or exercise regimen or other life changing venture until you identify the limiting factors that are preventing you from achieving those goals. I also encourage you to focus on finding the motivation to support those goals. One of my favorite take-aways was from John Assaraf who put into play an example of finding the motivation to make a million dollars. He said if you believe you cannot make a million dollars then it is because you haven't found the right motivation. Imagine a different circumstance, what if your child was kidnapped and you had to come up with a million dollars. Do you think you might be able to do it now? (26). The good news is you don't need a tragic motivation to achieve a goal, you just need a very strong and convincing one. Before starting any new routine that is difficult for you, spend some time finding or creating a motivation for yourself and overcoming (both physically or mentally) the limiting factors that prevent you from achieving those goals. Then start with your action steps. It is only when these things have been addressed that you will have the best chance to be successful.

Negative Space Identity

In the art world there is a painting technique called *painting by the use of negative space.* That is basically when instead of painting the object of interest, instead you draw or paint the space around the object of interest. It is another way to define your object. And it can have beautiful results. I think in our own life and health design, we should utilize this concept. One thing we must do is define ourselves. However, this is the easy part. We can easily choose to say anything about ourselves and so long as we stay in a completely sterile environment, then everything we think and believe about ourselves must be absolutely true. However, in reality we live in an environment of variable factors out of our control and what we would like to be true isn't always true when we apply external factors. So, we need to stabilize those parts of our identities by first drawing ourselves, but specifically by utilizing a negative space design. We must confirm our identities with the outside world not for ego sake but because our reality is a product of not only our internal self but of our self in relation to the external world. This may sound confusing but when I say confirm your identity with the outside world, I am not talking about looking for recognition. I am talking about creating an irrefutable fact internally and externally. When you have concreted your identity both internally and externally, then it is harder for those core concepts to be challenged by others and less likely to create conflict within ourselves and in our interactions with others. Again, I am talking about this knowledge of self so much and in so much detail, because ultimately this is the major distraction from challenges that require our full attention such as health problems.

Consider if you are using your computer and you open 100 different applications. Ideally each process should run smoothly, but similar to your own mind and body, running 100 different applications whether small or big will slow down the processing and often cause instability in the system. That is why we need to address our own chronic emotional and personal instabilities in order to deal with major illness. I can't say that we can be totally successful to focus on solely one issue given all the complexities of our minds, but at least if it is only a few issues, we will be much more efficient in addressing them. So, if it is important to you that you are a good dancer, perhaps enrolling in dance classes and eventually dance competitions can help you master a skill that represents a core concept for you. Then it will be very difficult for anyone to challenge that concept, because you will have much hard, real evidence to support your core foundations. This is another principle of what contributes to happiness. Do not let fears limit you. When you feel insecure about something, do your best to solidify your skill and preparedness in that particular area so that nothing can shake you. In life, our strengths take us places, but it is our weaknesses that others target in bringing us down. So, while we should utilize our strengths the most, it is important also to work on our weaknesses as well.

Understanding your Purpose and Passion

We spoke of the benefits of purpose and passion. How do you find out what they are if you don't already know? There are great methods for doing this that I will include in my upcoming workbook by way of self-questioning. But what is important to remember here is that your purpose and passion may not be the same. Most successful against all odds people will tell you that you should not follow money. You should follow your passion. But I can tell you that there are many people that follow passion that are never successful. We only hear of the ones that happen to be successful. I have known people that were passionate to become doctors. They took the entrance exams more than a few times, but could never pass. I have also known musicians that toured for many years and would not be considered successful though it was their passion. The truth is that there is a hidden component. I think that people who talk about following their passion forget to disclose that their passion happens to also be their purpose. Sometimes that can be the case. What distinguishes the two is that purpose must give us connection to our outer world. So if you are a musician who is able to connect with the world through music, then likely you will be successful. If you are unable to do that, even though it may be your highest passion, you will be unlikely to succeed. Therefore, your purpose requires you to also have a level of skill and ability to provide something to others and it must be something that most others do not have in that area.

In order to identify your purpose and passion, you must first understand your own strengths and weaknesses and which of those strengths and weaknesses gives you the ability to connect and do service for others. I mention weaknesses again here because often it is what mostly society considers a general weakness that has more potential to be a part of your greater purpose. My annoying nocturnal and late night habits which I struggled with ultimately turned into a very successful profession. It was something that people told me to fight against throughout my life. Early risers were encouraged in all school environments and especially in the medical field. Yet my nocturnal inclination was the most powerful tool I had as I later realized it was actually what set me apart.

In interviews, often they ask you what your strengths and weaknesses are. If you have ever had job interview training, they tell you that you should turn your negatives into positives. You state them without denial and then show how they might actually be positive. I encourage you to actually do this in real life. Embrace your negatives and channel them into a potential positive good (not everyone may see the good in them, but there may be opportunities out there somewhere). If you are fighter, teach people to defend themselves. If you are annoying, then be annoying for a good cause. If you cry a lot, cry with others so that they feel relief. My point is often those negatives are often the best part of us. We just fail to see it.

Once you have analyzed your strengths and weaknesses, look for ways those can help you connect with the world and a way you can be passionate about. It may not be your highest passion, but you can find a passion that will drive your purpose. See, your purpose should incorporate passion, skill, and connection. That is the combination that will create in you success. Passion and skill is what will set you apart, but it is the connection that will actually bring you the success. This is the part that most people do not understand. They live their art or their dreams in isolation and then wonder why they are not successful. Our power comes in our ability to share our gifts.

Beauty Lies in the Eyes of the Beholder

We spoke of positive perspectives earlier as a green zone principle. But what if I told you the following topic is one of the most important advanced skills to master. Not only is positive perspective important, but taking control of one's entire perspective is crucial. You have the power to change your perspective of life. Simple question. Would you rather be happy or sad? Why is that answer so obvious? It is obvious because almost all of us prefer to be happy. So why can't we be happy? Is it because of this or that or him or her or that health problem or this one?....Yes, there are a million justifications for why we choose not to be happy. But it is still our choice. If you want to be happy right now, you can. Would you rather be happy or sad? Happy, ok, so be happy as I always tell my son. Simply take a breath, smile, and feel that all the world is right, even your problems are as they should be. The more we do this, the more you will realize that the only thing causing you to be sad is you. And you can change this without a raise, without a promotion, without a better body, without a nicer house or car, without a better husband or wife, or without whatever problem you think is at the root of all your despair. You can simply choose to be and then be. That is the power of perspective. So, what prevents us from believing we can do this? Really, it is the loss of hope that causes us to believe we cannot change our perspective. Often people can be happy in less than ideal situations if they know it is only temporary or if it is part of their path to a better situation. Take for example my residency. Not many people would be happy about working 80 hours a week and getting paid less than minimum wage, and yet I recall it as one of the happiest times of my life. This was because I had great friends, our residency war scars bonded us and we laughed about the insanity of the whole thing. But all of us knew it would end at some point. It was not forever. If we had imagined that the situation of 36-hour shifts would continue for the rest of life, I doubt any of us would have recall that time with any degree of fondness. See how strong perspective really is in our lives.

In advanced techniques of Getting into the Green Zone, find out what viewpoints cause you sadness and distress. Then see if you can change those perspectives. Maybe your child cries a lot and it drives you crazy. But maybe they are a just a highly sensitive child who feels deeply and strongly and needs you to tell them that everything is ok. Perhaps your boss doesn't pay you as much as you want. But even so, you can remember that they are taking on the risks of a business and making sure you get a paycheck every month and feel grateful for their bravery. Perhaps your spouse is less than perfect. But perhaps you can accept imperfections in them just as they do with you. I am not telling you to settle, I am telling you to find contentment in your current situation. Change and growth will not be quashed by doing this, I promise. You will still be able to recognize that you need to be paid more and find a better job, and it is a natural inclination for humans to want more. That dissatisfaction guarantees our constant evolution. But we don't need to let it get to the point of hate and depression just so we can recognize a need to change. Instead, recognize those signs telling us that it is time to evolve, change, learn and grow. Those things are also a part of life, not just the happy, settled moments. When you have mastered this technique, then you will feel less severe emotions as times of difficulty and stress come into your life. You will accept them as a part of the wave of life, just as surfers know, eventually they must sometimes eat the waves. That is part of the process. Also, as you advance with this technique, you will be able to find hope easier in every situation, because you will begin to realize your own role in being able to change. Never does life have to continue forever in despair. You have the power to change your life right now as soon as you decide to do so. You may need to ask for help or create a plan you never thought of before, but your view of life is entirely in your own hands, even if you never realized it.

Delegation of Duty and Responsibility

Delegation is not just for business success, although that is where we typically consider the use of delegation. Delegation can apply to our personal life as well. Suppose you aren't able to address all your limiting issues for one of your health problems. Delegation is a great way to allow yourself focus on one issue. Consider if personally you know you have absolutely zero motivation to exercise. Then hiring a trainer removes the responsibility of you needing to create or invent a motivation. They will become your motivation. All you need to do is show up and follow their instruction. This resolves the mental processing of trying to exercise enough. It will take that burden from your mind and now perhaps you can just focus on your diet. Perhaps you are great at exercising, but your diet is not so great. Then perhaps hiring a service that sends you healthy meals will be a way to delegate away the responsibility of having to eat right. This is why it is very important to find out what your specific strengths and weaknesses are. If you know them, you can understand which tasks are best to delegate out to someone else and which to continue doing yourself. In my upcoming workbook, we will go through all these exercises in order to help us create what I call Prescription Plan for Life, which will help us more easily get into the green zone.

Gratefulness

Such a simple concept. A lot of people may think it silly. Based on actual research done in California and Florida and university institutions, gratefulness can increase happiness by at least 10%, (see the table below) simply by writing letters expressing your thankfulness weekly. These studies were conducted by top Psychologists in the country.

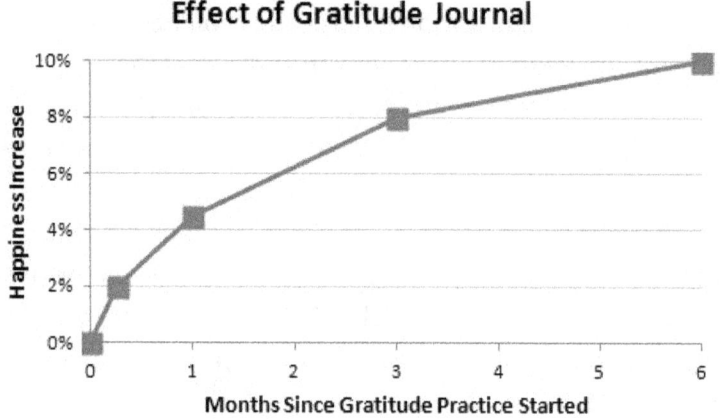

Doctors at UC Davis and The University of Miami found a relation between writing what you are thankful for and fewer doctor visits and higher exercise levels.

While it is difficult to prove these correlations, there is quite a bit of evidence to support that gratefulness can impact you in quantifiable measures (27).

Keeping a gratitude journal caused participants to report 16% fewer physical symptoms, 19% more time spent exercising, 10% less physical pain, 8% more sleep, and 25% increased sleep quality.	Counting Blessings Versus Burdens	2003
The emotions of appreciation and gratitude shown to induce the relaxation response.	The Grateful Heart	2004
A gratitude visit reduced depressive symptoms by 35% for several weeks; a gratitude journal lowered depressive symptoms by 30%+ for as long as the practice was continued.	Positive Psychology Progress	2005
Patients with hypertension were instructed to count their blessings once a week. There was a significant decrease in their systolic blood pressure.	Gratitude: Effects on Perspectives and Blood Pressure	2007
Gratitude correlated with improved sleep quality ($r = .29$), less time required to fall asleep ($r = .20$), and increased sleep duration ($r = .14$).	Gratitude Influences Sleep Through the Mechanism of Pre-Sleep Cognitions	2009
Levels of gratitude significantly correlated with vitality and energy.	Multiple Studies	Many

Other reported benefits are higher levels of success, improved test scores, and improved immune systems. So, practicing gratefulness is another Advanced Green Zone technique I want you to learn. Just to recap, practicing gratefulness not only increases happiness, but also decreases doctor visits. That is why I must strongly encourage the practice of gratefulness since it directly affects both the ultimate goals for you, better health and increased happiness.

As a note, it is shown that practicing gratefulness can also increase optimism. Remember when I said you should learn to have a more positive perspective, this is one tool by which you can do that. I want to emphasize that we generally have a set level of optimism and thankfulness that we live at as a rule. Oddly enough, this is not something we often choose for ourselves but again something we learned as children. Without conscious effort, we will always return to this preset level. Think of it as a thermostat. Our subconscious mind likes to operate efficiently, which means we utilize the most familiar processes to deal with day to day life. Your mind is designed to do go back to what is familiar in all senses. Know that you *can* change this with awareness. But if you ask why you are not that optimistic of a person to begin with, it is not your fault really. Don't focus on that, but on how you can change to become an optimist. Practicing gratefulness is a great start to that end.

Creating a Prescription Plan for Life

This may be a difficult task to undertake for oneself, but essentially this will be your master list of problems to address and bring you closer to a life of health and happiness. Try to tailor the list to incorporate Green Zone Principles. Order the problems by urgency and what brings highest levels of stress. Then address each problem one by one. Leave a section of less urgent issues to be addressed at your planning sessions or annual doctors' visits. As problems become solved, don't erase them from your list, but drop them down to the bottom, with a note on how they are being addressed. In the medical community, we do this a lot. For example, for coronary artery disease in a patient where there is not an acute problem, you would say, CAD—controlled with same regimen of Aspirin, diet control, and blood pressure controlling meds such as …. etc.

We do this because it is important to remember what conditions and issues we are dealing with as we treat other issues and conditions. It also helps remind us continually to reassess if we have truly optimized that particular topic. In like fashion, do the same with your Prescription Life Plan. On this list you can include any issues medical, emotional, relationship, physical, financial, or spiritual. It will give you a new way to structure how you do things and how you plan your life.

"It's not Easy Bein' Green"(28)

But what about the Chocolate, Doc?

Ok, yes, being part of a chocolate lovers club isn't easy when you are teaching principles of Green Zone living and promoting dietary recommendations that avoid refined and processed foods. Like I stated, this is a guideline to help you achieve your best optimal state of health. I too, love Taco Bell, and soda and pizza but I share this knowledge so that we all can achieve better living. I am not perfect nor do I expect everyone else to be perfect. I just encourage you to understand that with each good choice you make, you are closer to that goal of optimal health and with each bad choice, it takes you a bit further. I don't profess to be perfect and I have many years of bad habits to put behind me so I am not certain if I will make it into the Millennial club, and even still I have much change to institute. One of my hardest challenges is the social pressure of people and organizations that do not share these same values and goals. Perhaps that is why Blue Zone Communities do so well, because they do share those common goals and institute common healthy practices. I only am trying to bring awareness and trying to encourage you to continue striving for a better version of yourself. Moderate the bad habits and try to institute some of these Green Zone Principles. Perhaps by eating a few more vegetables and avoiding a few more desserts at least my son will have a better grasp of those principles than I did and live a bit longer and a bit happier than myself. This is also my wish for all my patients and their children or future children. I hope by sharing this information it will help myself, others, and society evolve in a positive way. Thanks for sharing in my journey. I hope it has been enlightening. Do more than just live, Live Well!

Appendices

I am including some fun facts and lists about happiness and a thought provoking movie list for your enjoyment.

Appendix A—Careers as per Forbes

Happiest Careers and their average salary (in the U.S. as of 2016)
1. Recruiter $56,715
2. Full Stack Developer $72,856
3. Research Assistant $31,624
4. Senior Java Developer $98,814
5. Android Developer $56,120
6. CTO $121,691
7. Lead Engineer $92,358
8. Lead Developer $82,296
9. Software QA Engineer $65,779
10. COO $125,086

Unhappiest Careers and their average salary (Forbes, 23).

1. Account Manager $65,414
2. Security Officer $26,603
3. Merchandiser $29,440
4. Cashier $19,685
5. Driver $39,098
6. Research Analyst $ 56147
7. Guard $36,218
8. Sales $50,000
9. Machine Operator $32,200
10. Service Technician $43,05

Appendix B---Places to Live:

Happiest Countries in the World

North American/European--

    Better Healthcare systems

    Higher income

    Better connectivity

    Relation to natural environment

Saddest Countries

African/Asian/Middle eastern--

    Low connectivity

    Low education

    Poor access to healthcare/vaccination

    Political/safety instability

Happiest States (Happiest from top to bottom)

1. Alaska

2. Hawaii

3. South Dakota

4. Wyoming

5. Montana

6. Colorado

7. Nebraska

8. Utah

9. New Mexico

10. Texas

Specifically, the list-topping happiest cities are Lafayette, Houma, Shreveport-Bossier City, Baton Rouge and Alexandria. (23).

Saddest States (#50 is considered Saddest)

41. Missouri

42. Michigan

43. Arkansas

44. Tennessee

45. Alabama

46. Mississippi

47. Ohio

48. Indiana

49. Kentucky

50. West Virginia

The unhappiest cities had New York City topping the list, followed by St. Joseph, Missouri; South Bend, Indiana; Erie, Pennsylvania; Evansville, Indiana–Henderson, Kentucky; Toledo, Ohio; Detroit, Michigan; Jersey City, New Jersey; Gary, Indiana; and Scranton–Wilkes-Barre–Hazleton, Pennsylvania. (23).

Appendix C—Green Zone Movies

List of 21 inspiring movies and why they are inspiring.

1. My All-American

    Many of us fear we do not have enough time to make a change, a difference, or an impact on the world. But it does not take that long, it could take a few weeks, a day, a month, or sometimes it only takes a moment. Remember this when you are afraid you are too late or don't have enough time.

2. Life of Pi

    Life is about perception. You cannot change reality or sometimes circumstance, but you can change perception instantly. And your perception is everything.

3. Last Holiday

    Bad things in life often happen to help you grow and to make you face the truth of your existence.

4. Pursuit of Happyness

    Fight and drive and determination are the keys to changing your life, and sometimes desperation is the motivating factor.

5. Instructions not Included

    Real love is what you determine it to be.

6. The Painted Veil

    How you define love is your decision.

7. Life is Beautiful

    Another movie about choosing your reality.

8. Sliding Doors

    Everything happens for a reason shown from another perspective

9. Under the Tuscan Sun

> Starting over is tough but can be a wonderfully exciting process

10. Karate Kid

> A poor financial state does not make you poor in spirit

11. Rudy

> Limitations are only present in your mind

12. Slumdog Millionaire

> Anyone can come out of impossible circumstances and also memory is a matter of storytelling

13. Kung Fu Panda 3

> You will never be anything but what you are, but that is the most powerful realization

14. The Lord of the Rings

> The constant struggle of good and evil exists within us all, we all have the possibility to be either one. At the end of the day it is a choice. When the choice is hard, you must think of the greater good.

15. Star Trek, The Search for Spock

> Love can exist in many forms. The value of one life is never to be underestimated.

16. Mrs. Doubtfire

> Finding a motivation is the key to enabling yourself to do anything.

17. Forrest Gump

> Courage is putting one foot in front of another and living in the present.

18. Me, Earl, and the Dying Girl

> Life is bigger than just you. And so is Death. Existence goes beyond yourself.

19. The Notebook

> Real love persists in both the good times and the bad times.

20. The Guardian

> Understanding a person's motivation is often key to helping yourself and the other person break through limitations and fears.

21. Extraordinary Measures

> How motivation is key to overcoming seemingly impossible obstacles.

References

1. (Buettner, The Blue Zones: Lessons for Living Longer From the People Who've Lived the Longest, 2008)

2. Future Oncol. Author manuscript; available in PMC 2011 Oct 1.Future Oncol. 2010 Dec; 6(12): 1863-1881. doi: 10.2217/fon.10.142 PMCID: PMC3037818 NIHMSID: NIHMS269073 Impact of stress on cancer metastasis; Myrthala Moreno-Smith, Susan K Lutgendorf, and Anil K Sood

3. http://adultdevelopment.wix.com/harvardstudy

4. The Oxford Companion to the Theatre entry under Green Room and the Rec.Arts.Theatre.Stagecraft newsgroup FAQ

5. http://sarahgershman.blogspot.com/2009/09/getting-in-green-room-zen-of-speaking.html

6. http://www.utne.com/community/thezenofsurfing

7. Segerstrom, Susan; Breaking Murphy's Law, How Optimists Get What They Want from Life-- and Pessimists Can Too

8. The Lancet Medical Journal Stressed brain, stressed heart?Ilze Bot,

9. http://www.possibilityoftoday.com/2010/12/06/10-secrets-of-the-happiest-people-in-the-world/

10. Sirgy, Joseph; The Psychology of Quality of Life: Hedonic Well-Being, Life Satisfaction, and Eudaimonia pp 115

11. http://www.apa.org/monitor/2011/12/exercise.aspx

12. Allen R McConnell Ph.D. The Social Self
    Friends with Benefits: Pets Make Us Happier, Healthier

13. The preference for experiences over possessions: Measurement and construct validation of the Experiential Buying Tendency Scale
    RT Howell, P Pchelin, R Iyer - The Journal of Positive Psychology, 2012 - Taylor & Francis

14. Jarden, A. (2012). Positive Psychologists on Positive Psychology: Robert Vallerand, International Journal of Wellbeing, 2(2), 125-130. doi:10.5502/ijw.v2i2.1

15. http://www.possibilityoftoday.com/2010/12/06/10-secrets-of-the-happiest-people-in-the-world/

16. https://authoritynutrition.com/dairy-and-cancer/

17. http://articles.mercola.com/sites/articles/archive/2016/05/07/too-much-protein-triggers-aging-cancer.aspx

18. https://www.bluezonesproject.com/

19. High-temperature beverages and Foods and Esophageal Cancer Risk -- A Systematic Review
Farhad Islami,[1,2,3] Paolo Boffetta,[2] JianSong Ren,[4] Leah Pedoeim,[4] Dara Khatib,[4] and Farin Kamangar[4]

20. http://www.heart.org/HEARTORG/HealthyLiving/HealthyEating/Nutrition/Alcohol-and-Heart-Health_UCM_305173_Article.jsp#.WOmfc2zHdhF

21. http://www.nwo.nl/en/research-and-results/cases/happiness-is-partly-in-your-genes.html

22. http://greatergood.berkeley.edu/article/item/the_childhood_roots_of_adult_happiness_an_annotated_bibliography

23. http://www.wnd.com/2014/07/5-happiest-cities-in-u-s-all-in-1-state/#RiOQjRmDfb6ZmuK2.99

24. https://www.forbes.com/sites/kathryndill/2016/03/04/the-happiest-and-unhappiest-jobs-in-2016/#5547d93bd796

25. Levitin, Daniel This Is Your Brain on Music: The Science of a Human Obsession Paperback - August 28, 2007

26. Assaraf, John. Having It All, audio dialogue conversation with caller.

27. Seligman , Martin Happier Human out of the University of Pennsylvania and Harvard, Effects of Gratefulness Table and graph.

28. Kermit the Frog, Quote Joe Raposo, originally performed by Jim Henson as Kermit the Frog, The Muppet Movie

About The Author

Dr. Jaya George-Fernandez Zavala is a fully trained Internal Medicine Physician recognized under the US American Board of Internal Medicine. She began at The Medical College of Georgia in Augusta, GA and completed her residency at The University of Southern California in Los Angeles, CA. She went on to work at a private group practice in Orange County, California. At the time of this book being published, she has spent over 14 years practicing medicine between both the East Coast and West Coast of the United States and has worked with hundreds of thousands patients of all classifications and walks of life, from prisoners to celebrities. She has worked in both a county medical system and a privatized medical system and helped patients both with insurance and without.

Her extensive experience has allowed her to identify trends and behaviors amongst patients and allows her a unique ability to create health strategy and optimization for individuals and organizations. She continues to have a great interest in coaching and helping people create life planning and strategies that will optimize their health and thus save them enormous time, energy, money, and prevent them from much suffering. She also works with youngsters to help them identify healthy career and life choices. She is the Best Selling and International author of the books *The Pregnancy Pocketbook* and *Getting Into The Green Zone* and is currently working on a follow up workbook.

She loves animals, ballroom dance, aromatherapy and harbors a special interest in music and loves studying applications of music in medicine. She takes an integrative approach to medicine utilizing her extensive background in Western Medicine and combines it with the long-standing tenets of mind-body connection from Eastern Medicine; integrating with them also neurolinguistics and neural reprogramming to create a state of the art health model that she calls *Dynamic Medicine* which allows individuals to achieve the highest quality of life possible.

www.ingramcontent.com/pod-product-compliance
Lightning Source LLC
Chambersburg PA
CBHW070255100426
42743CB00011B/2244